SEARCH ANALYTI
FOR YOUR SITE
CONVERSATIONS WITH YOUR CUSTOMERS

T0257657

Louis Rosenfeld

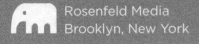

Rosenfeld Media
Brooklyn, New York

Search Analytics for Your Site: Conversations with Your Customers
By Louis Rosenfeld

Rosenfeld Media, LLC
457 Third Street, #4R
Brooklyn, New York
11215 USA

On the Web: www.rosenfeldmedia.com
Please send errors to: errata@rosenfeldmedia.com

Publisher: Louis Rosenfeld
Developmental Editor: Stephanie Zhong
Managing Editor: Marta Justak
Interior Layout Tech: Danielle Foster
Cover Design: The Heads of State
Indexer: Nancy Guenther
Proofreader: Chuck Hutchinson

© 2011 Rosenfeld Media, LLC
All Rights Reserved
ISBN: 1-933820-209
ISBN-13: 978-1-933820-20-0
LCCN: 2011907226

Printed and bound in the United States of America

DEDICATION

To Mary Jean, Iris, and Nate, who generously gave me the time to write this book.

And to my mother and father, whose talents at cheating time I hope to emulate.

HOW TO USE THIS BOOK

Who Should Read This Book?

I wrote this book primarily for user experience practitioners—the people who are responsible for a Web site or intranet's information architecture, content strategy, design, usability, and just about anything else that impacts a site's users. I especially wanted to help those practitioners see how analyzing searchers' behaviors is just another critical tool, like task analysis, personas, and field studies, that belongs in their user research toolkits.

There are also many people in the web analytics community who haven't turned their attention toward analyzing and improving site search. SSA belongs in their toolkit, so this book is for web analytics practitioners as well.

Honestly, if your Web site or intranet has its own search engine, then you should find *something* here that's worth at least the price of the book.

What's in This Book?

If you're new to SSA, read the first two chapters: they consist of a case study that demonstrates how SSA made a difference at The Vanguard Group and a quick one-chapter introduction to get you up and running.

If you're ready to jump right in, the second section is full of tools and approaches to help you get the most out of analyzing your query data. Chapters 3–6 will be especially helpful if you want to gain new insights from your data. Chapter 7 will help you use the data to measure how well your site is performing against the goals you've already determined for it.

The third section introduces some of the very practical ways to improve your search system's performance, as well as your site's navigation, metadata, and content. You can start trying—and benefiting from—many of these tips right away.

The last chapter takes a step back from site search analytics and looks at how its parent disciplines—user experience and web analytics—differ and ultimately complement each other in a surprisingly elegant way. If you're looking to bridge these disciplines within your own organization, this chapter provides advice, and I hope some inspiration. Spoiler alert: SSA might be just the thing to bring the two of them together.

Section One: Introducing Site Search Analytics

Chapter 1: Site Search Analytics in Action

Chapter 2: Site Search Analytics in a Nutshell

Section Two: Analyzing the Data

Chapter 3: Pattern Analysis

Chapter 4: Failure Analysis

Chapter 5: Session Analysis

Chapter 6: Audience Analysis

Chapter 7: Goal-Based Analysis

Section Three: Improving Your Site

Chapter 8: Practical Tips for Improving Search

Chapter 9: Practical Tips for Improving Navigation and Metadata

Chapter 10: Practical Tips for Improving Content

Section Four: Coda

Chapter 11: Bridging Web Analytics and User Experience

What Comes with this Book?

This book's companion Web site (AR http://rosenfeldmedia.com/books/searchanalytics/) contains some templates, discussion, and additional content related to site search analytics. You'll also find a calendar of my upcoming workshops and talks on site search analytics. I've also made the book's diagrams and other illustrations available under a Creative Commons license (when possible) for you to download and include in your own presentations. You can find these on Flickr at AR www.flickr.com/photos/rosenfeldmedia/sets/.

FREQUENTLY ASKED QUESTIONS

What is site search analytics (SSA)?

If your Web site or intranet has a search engine, then you can log what users are searching for, tally queries to see what's most important to your users, find out if they're succeeding, and if they're not, determine what might be getting in their way. Chapter 2 provides a short introduction to SSA (which is often also known as *search log analysis*).

Isn't SSA the same as SEO?

Not at all. Search engine optimization looks for ways to make *Web-wide searches* (for example, via Google and Bing) more likely to find your site. SSA looks for ways to improve how searching works *on your site,* using your site's own search engine. That said, SSA and SEO share much in common, and can influence each other; for example, pages 90–91 shows how SSA may help you determine better keywords to bid on.

How does SSA differ from other kinds of analytics?

SSA is based on data that comes from actual usage of your site, just like other forms of web analytics. But it's far more semantic, as it is made of search queries—users' expressions of what information they want from your site *in their own words.* That's why SSA does a better job of depicting and helping you understand users' intentions than any other form of web analytics. Chapter 3 provides some tools for analyzing and understanding users intentions.

Why do I need SSA?

Because SSA can help drive—and back up—your design decisions. Because you already have query data and want to put it to good use. Because you want to make your search engine find content better (Chapter 8), make your site easier to navigate (Chapter 9), and make your content more effective (Chapter 10). And because your competitors aren't using it, and you'd like to destroy your competitors.

Where does query data come from, and what tools do I need to analyze it?

When someone uses your site's search engine, they type a query that the engine will try to match with your site's content. That query can be (and likely is being) saved. It's either logged in a text file by your search engine or intercepted and kept in a database by your analytics application. Search engines occasionally and analytics tools increasingly provide reports that help you analyze the data, but ideally you'll explore and learn more from the data in a spreadsheet. Unfortunately, there's no one way to get your hands on the data, because how you can get at the data often depends on what search engine you're using. Talk to your organization's IT people for help and show them this book if they ask why you need access to the data.

I'm not a "data person," so why should I read this book?

Organizations are putting more and more pressure on designers to justify their decisions with evidence. Fortunately, SSA is real data that's also semantically rich, so you won't be just looking at numbers. And you won't need to perform statistical tests to learn from it; in fact, it will be immediately obvious to you how it can help improve your design work

This isn't part of my job description (or anyone else's) so who should do this work?

User researchers and the designers who rely upon user research—such as information architects, content strategists, interaction designers, and knowledge managers—should at least consider SSA as a part of their standard kits of research tools, even if it's not something they use on a regular basis. The same goes for web analytics practitioners: SSA is an important tool, just like clickstream analysis. The best part is that no one needs to do SSA as a job—it scales nicely, depending on the time you have available (see our discussion of the Zipf Distribution on pages 19–21).

How do I actually analyze query data?

First, "play" with the data by looking for patterns and surprises that suggest what's important to your searchers and what kinds of content will best meet their needs (Chapter 3). Then identify and learn from searchers' failures (Chapter 4). See what happens in the course of single search sessions (Chapter 5), and tease out what's important to specific audiences of searchers (Chapter 6). Finally, measure your site's performance better by injecting search metrics into how your site is performing at meeting its goals (Chapter 7).

How does SSA fit with other user research methods?

SSA is based mostly on quantitative behavioral data; therefore, it's useful to combine it with your qualitative user research methods and tools. For example, use query data to help determine candidates' tasks for your task analysis studies or to beef up your personas with real data. Chapter 11 talks about how SSA fits into the broader worlds of both user experience research and web analytics, and how it may be a great means for bringing them together.

If it's so great, how come more people aren't taking advantage of SSA?

Good question. Most people don't know that query data even *exists,* much less that their organizations likely already own some. Those who do often run into political problems when they try to get their hands on the data, because it is usually owned by IT or some other group. (This is getting easier thanks to ever-improving analytics tools.) Finally, there hasn't been much practical information on how to analyze the data. Maybe this book will help.

TABLE OF CONTENTS

How to Use This Book   iv

Who Should Read This Book?   iv
What's in This Book?   iv
What Comes with this Book?   v

Frequently Asked Questions   vi

Foreword   xiv

SECTION ONE

Introducing Site Search Analytics

CHAPTER 1

How Site Search Analytics Can
Save Your Butt   1

The Brake Gets Pulled   2
The Brake Gets Stuck   3
Measuring the Unmeasurable   4
The Before-and-After Test   5
The Brake Works—
    Thanks to Site Search Analytics   9
Moral of the Story: Be Like John   12

CHAPTER 2

Site Search Analytics in a Nutshell   13

What Is Site Search Analytics?   14
Why You'll Want to Use SSA   16
It Always Starts with Data   16
George Kingsley Zipf, Harvard Linguist
    and Hockey Star   19

Ways to Use SSA (and This Book)   22

What Gets in the Way of SSA?   23

Who Is Responsible for SSA?   25

Your Secret Weapon   26

Summary   32

SECTION TWO

Analyzing the Data

CHAPTER 3

Pattern Analysis

Pattern Analysis   33

Analysis as a Form of Play   34

Getting Started with Pattern Analysis   36

Patterns to Consider   40

Finding Patterns in the Long Tail   52

Anti-Pattern Analysis: Surprises and Outliers   55

Summary   60

CHAPTER 4

Failure Analysis

Failure Analysis   61

Study Failure with Care   62

Queries That Return Zero Results   63

Queries That Fail to Retrieve Useful Results   68

Queries That Lead to Immediate Exits from the Site   72

Beyond Generic—Evaluating Failures

   That Mean the Most   74

Summary   77

CHAPTER 5
Session Analysis

Session Analysis	79
Learning from Who Searched What and When	80
Why Analyze Sessions?	83
What's a Session, Anyway?	83
Analyzing a Short Session from TFANet	84
Analyzing a Long Session from WW Norton	86
Which Sessions Should You Analyze?	89
How Granular Are Your Terms?	90
Going Beyond Sessions: Looking at Individual Searchers	92
Summary	94

CHAPTER 6
Audience Analysis

Audience Analysis	95
Why Segment Your Audience?	96
How to Segment Your Audience	99
Comparing and Contrasting Segments	104
What's Next?	106
Summary	107

CHAPTER 7
Goal-Based Analysis

Goal-Based Analysis	109
Goal Tracking Is Good, but Search Metrics Make It Better	110
Determining Goals and KPIs	113
Summary	119

SECTION THREE
Improving Your Site

CHAPTER 8
Practical Tips for Improving Search   121

Plugging Gaps in Your Search Engine's Index   122
Making Query Entry Easier by Fixing "the Box"   122
Accommodating Strange Query Syntax   124
Determining What Your Best Bets Should Be   126
Helping Searchers Auto-Complete
   Their Queries   127
Improving a "No Results Found" Page   129
Helping Searchers Revise Their Queries to
   Get Better Results   130
Designing Search Results Around Specialized
   Query Types   132
Designing Search Results Around Specialized
   Content Types   137
Summary   142

CHAPTER 9
Practical Tips for Improving
Site Navigation and Metadata   143

Improving Contextual Navigation for Specific
   Content Types   144
Creating a Better Site Index   148
Testing and Tuning Metadata Values Important   150
Summary   154

CHAPTER 10
Practical Tips for Improving Content

Practical Tips for Improving Content   155

Determining Which Content You Should Get Rid of   156
Plugging Content Gaps   156
Making Relevant Content Even More Relevant   158
Expanding Your Understanding of Users'
    Content Interests   159
Getting Marketing to Do the Right Thing   161
Getting Content Owners to Do the Right Thing   162
Summary   164

SECTION FOUR
Coda

CHAPTER 11
Bridging Web Analytics and User Experience

Bridging Web Analytics and User Experience   165

Data and Design: Never the Twain Shall Meet   166
The Case for Integrated Problem Solving   168
Persona Chart:
    Steven (Contractor)   173

Creating a Single User Research Brain Within
    Your Organization   177
Site Search Analytics: The Natural Boundary Object   182

Index   185

Acknowledgments   195

About the Author   199

FOREWORD

 A funny thing happened the first time Lou and I teamed up to teach our day-long public workshops (mine on usability, his on information architecture), probably eight years ago now.

I went to his workshop—the day before mine—partly out of due diligence, but mostly because I've always enjoyed listening to Lou, and I knew I'd learn a lot.

Halfway through the day, Lou spent 10 minutes talking about something I think he called "search log analysis" at the time. Basically, you get your hands on the log data for your site's search engine so you can see what terms people are searching for most often. Then you take the most-searched-for items (say, the top 25) for the current month, execute the searches yourself, and see what you can learn from them.

For instance:

- **Were there any results?** If not, maybe you need to add content, or at least figure out why people on your site are looking for something you don't have.

- **If there were results, were they the best content your site has on the topic?** If not, you may want to tweak your search engine or fiddle with some keywords.

- **And why were people using Search to find these things?** Was it because it's not obvious how to get to them through your navigation?

Basically, Lou was suggesting that you spend a very small amount of time each month to see if people are finding the things they're looking for on your site. Then you tweak your navigation, your content, or your search engine as needed to make sure they can. The next month, you do it again, with the new top 25.

The funny thing was that I'd been making *almost exactly the same speech* in my workshops for a long time, pretty much word for word.

When I mentioned it to Lou later, it turned out that even though the technique was really off-topic for both of our workshops, we both thought that we just had to tell people about it, because we thought it was *the* most cost-effective thing people could do to improve their site. Very little effort, very big payoff, and almost no skills required. And virtually no one knew about it.

Fast-forward, several years.

Besides starting up a publishing company, having two great kids, and relocating from Ann Arbor to Brooklyn, Lou decided to write a book. About this topic. Which he now called *Site Search Analytics*.

Fast-forward several more years to today, when you're holding the book in your hands. (Or reading it on a digital device that didn't exist when this all started.)

Lucky you. You get the benefit of years of pondering, researching, inventing, and fine-tuning by somebody as smart as Lou. (In this case, Lou.)

One caution: Don't be intimidated by the soup-to-nuts scope of the book. Even though Lou spells out a lot that you can do, you don't have to absorb (or even read; sorry, Lou) all of it. I encourage you to just try a little bit; dip a toe in the water, if you will.

With nothing more than this book, a few hours of your time, and perhaps a copy of Excel, you'll be amazed at how much better your site can be.

And once you see how much you can learn in a few hours, don't be surprised if you get hooked and want to do a lot more. That's when you'll be glad Lou wrote the whole book.

Have fun.

—Steve Krug
   Author, *Don't Make Me Think!* and *Rocket Surgery Made Easy*

I love internal site search data. Completely.

My love emanates from a singular fact: Of all the data we have access to, site search is the only place where we have direct access to visitor intent.

When people click on links to visit your Web site, you know the sites or search engines they come from. How much intent does that communicate to you? 10%. It is really hard to know from that data *why* people might be showing up. How much intent is there in the keywords that people type into search engines like Google, Bing, or Baidu? Maybe a bit more than 10%, but honestly not that much. Our beloved visitors are notorious for being deliberately vague when they use search engines.

Yet when people search Web sites, they become astonishingly precise about why they are there. The queries they type into site search engines contain oodles of intent, just waiting for us to convert into insights that drive greater customer satisfaction.

Over the last couple of years, it's been amazing to see how much valuable intent data is now available from almost all analytics tools, including Google Analytics. What words did people type? How many of them left your site because search results were so horrible? How many people had to refine their queries to get your search engine to cough up the right answer? Is there a material difference between conversion rates for people who use site search users and those who don't? With site search analytics, all these questions and more can now be more easily answered.

So now that the data is available, how does your site go from merely okay to magnificently glorious? That's where this lovely book by Lou comes into play.

Gently holding your hands, whispering soothing words, Lou will guide you through this rich and untapped world. You'll start simple: just reading

Chapter 2 will bring you 10x the return on what you paid for the book. Subsequent chapters will take you deeper and empower you to answer invaluable questions. How do you understand the patterns in your data (Chapter 4)? How do you analyze the audience (Chapter 7)? How do you achieve the nirvana of bridging the world of quantitative and the qualitative (Chapter 11)? All will be revealed using real-world examples, practical actionable tips, and a precision that will yield immediate benefit to your website visitors (and long-term benefits to your own salary!).

Carpe Diem!

—Avinash Kaushik
  Author, *Web Analytics 2.0* and *Web Analytics: An Hour A Day.*

CHAPTER 1

How Site Search Analytics Can Save Your Butt

The Brake Gets Pulled   2

The Brake Gets Stuck   3

Measuring the Unmeasurable   4

The Before-and-After Test   5

The Brake Works—Thanks to Site Search Analytics   9

Moral of the Story: Be Like John   12

I could jump right into telling you all about site search analytics—after all, that's the goal of the book. But a story might be a bit more instructive and interesting way to introduce the topic. So let's start with a true story of how one large organization faced a grave problem with its search system—and how site search analytics saved the day, as well as some jobs.

The Brake Gets Pulled

John Ferrara should have been satisfied.

After all, his employer, financial services giant The Vanguard Group, had just purchased a powerful new search engine to make its intranet's content searchable. Given its long history of investing in user experience, the company had asked John, an information architect on the staff, to help select the new engine and ensure that it served the end users. And, unlike many organizations, The Vanguard Group actually listened to its information architect's advice. The installation was going swimmingly, and the technology seemed to be working. The search engine was running on a development server, the launch was scheduled, and it wouldn't be long before Vanguard's 12,000 employees were enjoying a far better search experience.

And yet, something didn't seem quite right.

The project manager wanted to ensure the quality of the search results and asked John to do a review of the build on the development server. So he poked around and kicked the new engine's tires, trying out a few common search queries to see what happened.

What happened wasn't pretty. The search engine seemed to be retrieving results that made no sense; the results were far worse, in fact, than those of its predecessor. How on earth could all that time, money, and effort lead to an even *worse* search experience?

The launch deadline loomed just a few weeks out.

The Brake Gets Stuck

So John pulled the chain to halt the process from going forward. With his project manager's support, John described the problem to the IT staff who owned the project. They nodded their heads and listened patiently. And then they told John that they couldn't see the problem. After all, the search engine was up and running, and had been set up as the vendor suggested. The vendor was experienced and clearly knew what it was doing, likely far more than anyone at Vanguard (John included) could possibly know about how a search engine should work. Anecdotal findings from one person's poor search experience weren't going to trump that knowledge. With the launch date just around the corner, the staff weren't about to halt the project.

Now, this may seem to be an unreasonable response. But most IT people would react in the same way, and with good reasons: *technically*, the search engine really was working quite well. And while Vanguard's IT staff were uncommonly sensitive to user experience issues, it wasn't clear that the problem John was intuiting actually existed. After all, he had no compelling proof to present that the search was broken. Combine these reasons with the pressures IT faced to get the project completed on schedule, and you could argue that the IT people were actually being very reasonable.

But as an information architect, John was concerned about the user experience of search. That's why he'd been brought in to the search engine selection process in the first place—to make sure that the search engine actually served the end user, rather than just conforming to a set of technical requirements. But the new search engine already seemed too likely to fail miserably. John could already envision the hate mail coming in from users who were demanding that the old search engine be reinstated. And he could already hear the words from managers' mouths: "What the hell happened here?" John had raised a red flag, but he failed to make a convincing argument.

So John wasn't satisfied. He'd tried to put the brakes on the search engine's launch to avert a disaster and had failed.

Measuring the Unmeasurable

Of course, John wasn't going to give up. Otherwise, this story would be a very boring way to kick off a book! Besides, a large IT investment—and people's jobs—were at stake.

When John first started working on the project, his goal was to introduce user-centered thinking to the search engine selection process to complement the technical tests that IT would be using. To do so in an environment that was both technical and, as a corporation, driven by the bottom line, he had to wade into some treacherous waters—he'd have to come up with some metrics to quantify the experience of using the current search engine.

Now you might wonder what the big deal was. Either the search engine found the damned thing, or it didn't—should be pretty easy to measure, right? Well, not quite.... There certainly are searches that work that way, for example, looking up a colleague's phone number in the Vanguard staff directory. But many—probably most—searches don't have a single "right" answer. "Parking," "benefits," and "experts" are all common queries on the Vanguard Intranet. They are also questions that have many answers— some more right than the others, but none that are ideal or perfect. From the perspective of users, *relevance* is very often *relative*.

Most designers know that it's difficult to measure search performance and, well, just about any aspect of the user experience. In fact, being asked to do so causes droplets of sweat to form on many a designer's brow. It just doesn't feel right. Experience is difficult to boil down to a few simple, measurable actions. Considering that most of those in the field don't have advanced degrees in statistics—and probably experienced similarly sweaty moments during high school algebra—it's not surprising.

Yet, here was John Ferrara, with a bachelor's degree in communications, sallying forth to measure the user experience of Vanguard's search system.

The Before-and-After Test

John focused on analyzing a few really common search queries to see how
well they were performing—queries that represented needs that huge
numbers of Vanguard's intranet searchers wanted addressed. If you're
familiar with the "long tail,"[1] these would be considered the "short head."
(If you're not, don't worry—you'll learn the basics in Chapter 2, "Site
Search Analytics in a Nutshell.") John wanted to compare how well these
queries performed before and after—with the original search system and
now with the new one.

Next, John needed some metrics for these common queries so he could
compare them. He knew that there wasn't a single metric that would
be perfect, so he hedged his bets and came up with two sets of metrics
respectively: *relevancy* and *precision*.[2] Relevancy measured how well
the search engine returned a query's best match at the top of all results.
Precision measured how relevant the top results were. (To be fair, John
didn't invent precision; he borrowed it from the information retrieval
researchers, who have been using it for years.) Let's take a closer look at
these two sets of metrics and how John used them.

So What's Relevant?

John went through his list of common search queries. To test how relevant
each would be, he had to make an informed judgment (also known as a *guess*)
at what a reasonable searcher would want to find for each query. *Reasonable*,
as in the results don't seem like they were selected by a crazy person.

We've already seen one good example of such a situation: finding a
colleague's phone number in the staff directory. There's a clear, obvious,
and correct answer to this question. But in many cases where the answer
wasn't so obvious, John got out his red pen and deleted those queries from
his relevancy test. He was now working with a cleaned-up set of queries
that he was confident had "right answers"—ones like "company address."

---

1   Chris Anderson's excellent book *The Long Tail* (Hyperion, 2006) described the long tail
    phenomenon and its impact on commerce sites like Amazon and Netflix.

2   In web analytics, these are referred to as accuracy and precision.

John determined the best matches for each remaining query. He then tested each query by recording where the best match ranked among the search results. Then he measured performance a few different ways. Was it the first result? If not, did it make the top five "critical" results? Each of these measurements had something to say about how well queries were performing. They helped in two ways: they revealed outliers that were problematic, and they helped track overall search system performance over time. Figure 1.1 shows the former: queries, such as "job descriptions" that have high numbers stand out problematically from their peers and deserve some attention.

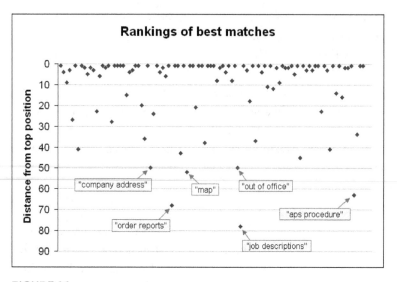

FIGURE 1.1

In a relevancy test, queries ideally find most reasonable results at position #1 on the search results page. A large distance from the top position suggests a poorly performing query.

John's relevancy test turned out to be very helpful. As Figure 1.1 shows, we can see which queries weren't retrieving their ideal result at or near the top of the search engine results page.

Yet there are two major limitations with relevancy testing: First, it leaves out many queries that don't have a "right answer"—queries that might be common and important. Second, this method relies on guessing what would be "right" for searchers, so it is a highly subjective measure. But a simple test like this one is a good starting point. It is consistent, and though it involves some subjective evaluation, it does so within a consistent framework. In this case, it allowed John to generate some simple test results from a representative sample. If the search engine failed this test—as Vanguard's did—then you have some serious problems (which they did).

Precision: Getting Beyond Relevance

That's why John decided to also introduce another set of metrics: precision. Precision measures the number of relevant search results divided by the total number of search results. It tells you how many of the search engine's results are good ones. John specifically looked at the precision of the top five results—the critical ones that a searcher would likely scan before giving up.

To test precision, John developed a scale for rating each result that a tested query retrieved, based on the information the searcher provided.

- **Relevant (r):** The result's ranking is completely relevant.

- **Near (n):** The result is not a perfect match, but it's clearly reasonable for it to be ranked highly.

- **Misplaced (m):** It's reasonable for the search engine to have retrieved the result, but it shouldn't be ranked highly.

- **Irrelevant (i):** The result has no apparent relationship to the query.

Rather than guessing at what the searcher's intent was, John was simply looking to assess how reasonable it was for the search engine to return each result, and whether or not the search engine put it in the right place. He recorded an r, n, m, or i for each result in a spreadsheet, as shown in Figure 1.2.

	A	B	C	D	E	F
1	Query string	Result 1	Result 2	Result 3	Result 4	Result 5
2	reserve room	r	n	n	r	m
3	software install	n	m	n	i	i
4	personal plan	m	n	i	i	n
5	pto	r	n	n	m	n
6	united way	m	m	m	m	m
7	visitor	m	i	n	r	n
8	morgan galley	r	r	m	n	n
9	referral	m	n	m	i	i
10	large transaction	m	i	i	i	i
11	closed funds	m	m	i	n	i
12	key request	r	m	n	m	i
13	irvs	m	m	m	n	m
14	holidays	r	m	m	i	n
15	ship shape	r	n	n	r	n
16	training	m	i	m	i	n

FIGURE 1.2
Each result for each query was rated as Relevant, Near, Misplaced, or Irrelevant.

John then used a few different ways to calculate precision for each query. He came up with three simple standards—strict, loose, and permissive—to reflect a range of tolerances for different levels of precision.

- **Strict:** Only results ranked as *relevant* were acceptable (r).

- **Loose:** Both *relevant* and *near* results were counted (r+n).

- **Permissive:** *Relevant, near,* and *misplaced* results were counted (r+n+m).

You can see how each query scored differently for each of these three precision standards in Figure 1.3. For example, of the first five search results for the query "reserve room," two were relevant (r), two were nearly relevant (n), and one was misplaced (m). In *strict* terms, precision was 40% (two of five results were relevant); in *loose* terms, 80% (four of five were relevant or nearly relevant); and all were relevant in *permissive* terms.

	A	B	C	D	E	F	G	H	I
1	Query string	Result 1	Result 2	Result 3	Result 4	Result 5	Precision (strict)	Precision (loose)	Precision (permissive)
2	reserve room	r	n	n	r	m	40%	80%	100%
3	software install	n	m	n	i	i	0%	40%	60%
4	personal plan	m	n	i	i	n	0%	40%	60%
5	pto	r	n	n	m	n	20%	80%	100%
6	united way	m	m	m	m	m	0%	0%	100%
7	visitor	m	i	n	r	n	20%	60%	80%
8	morgan galley	r	r	m	n	n	40%	80%	100%
9	referral	m	n	m	i	i	0%	20%	60%
10	large transaction	m	i	i	i	i	0%	0%	20%
11	closed funds	m	m	i	n	i	0%	20%	60%
12	key request	r	m	n	m	i	20%	40%	80%
13	irvs	m	m	m	n	m	0%	20%	100%
14	holidays	r	m	m	i	n	20%	40%	80%
15	ship shape	r	n	n	r	n	40%	100%	100%
16	training	m	i	m	i	n	0%	20%	60%

FIGURE 1.3

Each query's precision scores were then calculated in three different ways: Strict, Loose, and Permissive.

The Brake Works—
Thanks to Site Search Analytics

John's two tests of the original search engine—*relevancy* and *precision*—yielded two sets of corresponding metrics that helped his team compare the new engine's performance against the old one (shown in Figure 1.4). The five relevancy metrics above the line were all based on how close to the top position the "ideal search result" placed. So the smaller the number, the better. For the "Target"—the benchmark figures based on the *old* search engine—the top queries' ideal results placed, on average, three places below #1, where they ideally would have been displayed. John looked at the same data in different ways, using a median count, and three percentages that showed how often the ideal result was below the #1, #5, and #10 positions, respectively.

John used different metrics for precision as well—the strict, loose, and permissive measures described previously. In this case, bigger numbers were better because they meant a higher percentage of the top five results were relevant. As mentioned, the "Target" scores were the benchmark; they showed how the old search engine was performing. And the "Oct 3" scores showed how the new search engine was performing. The verdict, as you can see in Figure 1.4, was not pretty.

Relevancy scores (Lower numbers are better)		
Ranking of the best match:	Target	Oct 3
Average distance from 1st	3	13 ●
Median distance from 1st	2	7 ●
How often below 1st?	47%	84% ●
How often below 5th?	12%	58% ●
How often below 10th?	7%	38% ●
Precision scores (Higher numbers are better)		
Quality of the top 5 results:	Target	Oct 3
By the strict standard	42%	15% ●
By the loose standard	71%	38% ●
By the permissive standard	96%	55% ●

FIGURE 1.4
The new search engine ("Oct 3") performed worse than the old one ("Target") for each metric.

Ouch. The numbers didn't lie—the new search engine, first measured on October 3, was performing worse on each metric than the old engine!

John and his project manager now had the proof they needed to convince the IT folks that the new engine's poor performance wasn't just something that came to him after a hard night of partying. The problem was real and serious, dire enough that he thought people could lose their jobs if the new search engine launched as is. IT responded accordingly. While the staff still were obligated to make the same launch deadline, they eliminated some planned features in favor of fixing the problem. Over the coming weeks, they identified the sources of the problems. The primary culprit—a misconfigured configuration file that was missed by Vanguard's search engine consultant—was fortunately a fairly simple fix. And it wouldn't have been detected without site search analytics.

You can see how their work progressed to the point where, by launch, they'd at least come close to getting the new search engine (as of October 16) to work about as well as the old one for each of the eight metrics, as shown in Figure 1.5.

Relevancy scores (Lower numbers are better)				
Ranking of the best match:	Target	Oct 3	Oct 10	Oct 16
Average distance from 1st	3	13 ●	7 ●	5 ○
Median distance from 1st	2	7 ●	3 ○	1 ●
How often below 1st?	47%	84% ●	62% ○	58% ◐
How often below 5th?	12%	58% ●	38% ◑	14% ○
How often below 10th?	7%	38% ●	10% ○	7% ●
Precision scores (Higher numbers are better)				
Quality of the top 5 results:	Target	Oct 3	Oct 10	Oct 16
By the strict standard	42%	15% ●	36% ○	39% ◔
By the loose standard	71%	38% ●	53% ◑	65% ○
By the permissive standard	96%	55% ●	72% ○	92% ○

FIGURE 1.5
As the launch date approached, the new search engine's performance improved dramatically—to the point where it had caught up with the old engine's performance.

So John's gut reaction was validated, and he had the numbers to back up his argument that some hard work was in line before the new engine launched. The search experience was measured, a problem was recognized and identified, the search engine was fixed, firings were averted, and egg-on-face was avoided. Since the launch, Vanguard has continued to monitor these metrics and fine-tune the engine's performance accordingly. It's now performing much, much better than the original search engine. And that's where our happy story ends.

Moral of the Story: Be Like John

There's an important takeaway from this case study: that UX practitioners and other designers should not only pay more attention to the numbers, but it's their *responsibility* to employ quantitative approaches to research and evaluate the user experience. If no one at Vanguard had taken on this responsibility, the entire project might have failed miserably.

And though it's not a lesson, there's another important point worth remembering: this is just the tip of the SSA iceberg. There's much more that can and should be done with your site's search query data.

In this book, I'll cover many of the ways you can use SSA to better align your site with your business strategy, and I'll show you how SSA can be used to diagnose problems with your site's content, metadata, navigation, and search system performance. I'll do my best to help you integrate SSA, which is an inherently data-driven way to analyze user behavior, into traditional, more qualitative user-centered design methodologies. SSA is a missing link and a goldmine of untapped riches for all kinds of designers. I hope my book will serve as a toolkit to help you mine the data and, like John, achieve a truly better user experience.

CHAPTER 2

Site Search Analytics in a Nutshell

What Is Site Search Analytics?   14
Why You'll Want to Use SSA   16
It Always Starts with Data   16
George Kingsley Zipf, Harvard Linguist
    and Hockey Star   19
Ways to Use SSA (and This Book)   22
What Gets in the Way of SSA?   23
Who Is Responsible for SSA?   25
Your Secret Weapon   26
Summary   32

I n the last chapter, I showed how Vanguard used (and continues to use) site search analytics to measure, monitor, and optimize its search system's performance. Not to mention that it improves the overall user experience, as well as saves money, promotes jobs, and avoids disaster. Now it's your turn to give it a try. The bulk of this book will teach you the nuts and bolts of SSA. Starting with Chapter 3, "Pattern Analysis," I'll show you how to analyze your data, gain actionable insights, and put them to good use so your organization can enjoy some of the same benefits as Vanguard. But before we go deep, we'll go broad. In this chapter, I'll briefly cover the nuts-and-bolts aspects of SSA: what it is, how it works, and why you would use it. Think of this chapter as an introduction to SSA in 20 pages or fewer.

What Is Site Search Analytics?

Site search analytics is, at its simplest, the analysis of the search queries entered by users of a specific search system (see Figures 2.1 and 2.2). What did they search? What do their searches tell you about them and their needs? How did their searches go? Does their experience suggest fixes or improvements to your site? Or does it raise follow-up questions to pursue through other forms of user research?

Note that in this book, we're exploring the searching performed on a Web site or intranet. We are *not* covering how people search the entire Web using Google or another search engine. There are certainly parallels, but as you'll see in the table in Figure 2.3, they're not the same; Referral Queries of the Michigan State University site came from Web search engines like Google; Local Queries were executed on MSU's own search engine.

	Search Term	None	Total Unique Searches
1.	salary		188
2.	portfolio		107
3.	resume		101
4.	contract		94
5.	pictograms		76
6.	experience design		72
7.	salary survey		72
8.	graphic design		71
9.	jobs		70
10.	pictogram		63

FIGURE 2.1
In SSA, you can analyze queries, like these frequent queries of the *AIGA.org* site, as reported by Google Analytics...

FIGURE 2.2

...to learn about what your users want from your sites and your organizations.

Michigan State University, September 2006

Referral Queries			Local Queries				
Query	Count	Percent	Query	Count	Percent		
michigan state	39165	21.33%	football	5891	1.24%		
msu	17940	9.77%	library	5382	1.13%		
michigan state	17357	9.45%	campus+map	3897	0.82%		
msu.edu	5251	2.86%	angel	3891	0.82%		
(other)	3958	2.16%	im+west	3847	0.81%		
campus map	2137	1.16%	map	3794	0.80%	MSU name	
www.msu.edu	1898	1.03%	study+abroad	3490	0.73%	sports	
map	1723	0.94%	football+sched	3122	0.66%	map	
michigan	880	0.48%	spartantrak	2689	0.57%	surprises	
spartan stadiu	871	0.47%	olin	2545	0.54%		
mp3,http://ww	853	0.46%	computer+sto	2292	0.48%		
michigan state	829	0.45%	chemistry	2048	0.43%		
maps	635	0.35%	cata	1981	0.42%		
michigan sta	635	0.35%	spartan+trak	1904	0.40%		
honors college	542	0.30%	registrar	1832	0.39%		
michigan state	482	0.26%	payroll	1826	0.38%		
nursing	428	0.23%	stuinfo	1815	0.38%		
scopes trial	396	0.22%	human+resou	1741	0.37%		
how to write a	378	0.21%	housing	1636	0.34%		
michigan univ	377	0.21%	ion+capa	1626	0.34%		
irgp	361	0.20%	jobs	1623	0.34%		
scopes monke	344	0.19%	wharton+cent	1591	0.33%		
margaret san	344	0.19%	capa	1573	0.33%		
dupont analys	330	0.18%	athletics	1555	0.33%		
msu map	308	0.17%	im+east	1531	0.32%		

FIGURE 2.3

Rich Wiggins of Michigan State University assembled, categorized, and even color-coded the most frequent queries from the open Web versus those generated locally to illustrate their differences.

Unlike people searching the Web, your site's searchers typically have more specific needs. They also may be familiar with your organization, its products, and its content—after all, they had to find their way to your site in order to use its search system. So the knowledge you'll glean from SSA will be a bit different than (and complementary to) what you'll learn from SEO (Search Engine Optimization) and SEM (Search Engine Marketing). Consider this analogy: if people searching the Web are essentially the leads you want to attract, people searching your site are the customers you hope to retain.

Why You'll Want to Use SSA

SSA is unique: there truly is nothing like studying what people want from your site. It should be in your research toolkit—not by itself, mind you—but there's no reason for it not to be there, unless your site somehow doesn't have a search system.

There are plenty of ways you can track and learn from users' behaviors aside from SSA. For example, if you're a web analytics person, you might rely on clickstream analysis; if you're a user researcher, perhaps you perform eye-tracking studies. They'll all tell you something about user intent.

But none of these methods will tell you what users want *in their own words.* SSA provides an unmatched trove of *semantic richness*—not just what users want, but the tone and flavor of the language they use to express those needs. And it's without the biases introduced by testing and a lab environment. Plus, you have the data already. You certainly won't find it anywhere else or acquire it any other way.

It Always Starts with Data

SSA starts with raw data that describes what happens when a user interacts with a search system. It's ugly, and we'll break it down shortly, but here's what it typically looks like (this sample is from the Google Search Appliance):

```
XXX.XXX.X.104 - - [10/Jul/2006:10:25:46 -0800] "GET
/search?access=p&entqr=0&output=xml_no_dtd&sort=date%3AD%3AL%3Ad1&ud=1&site=All
Sites&ie=UTF-8&client=www&oe=UTF-
8&proxystylesheet=www&q=lincense+plate&ip=XXX.XXX.X.104 HTTP/1.1" 200 971 0
0.02
```

This data gets captured in a search log file—something your site's search engine likely does automatically. Or the search activity gets intercepted, like other analytics data, by a snippet of JavaScript code embedded in each page and template. The intercepted data then gets stored in a database. That's how Google Analytics, Omniture, Unica, and other analytics applications do it. You really don't need to know much about how this code works, but now you can at least claim to have seen it.

```
<script type="text/javascript" src="http://www.google-analytics.com/urchin.js ">

</script><script type="text/javascript">_uacct = "UA-xxxxxx-x"urchinTracker();

</script>
```

Although search engines and your analytics application may gather search data, they're traditionally and disappointingly remiss at providing reports on site search performance. Even when they do, you still may want to get at the raw data to analyze and learn things that the reports—which tend to be quite generic—won't tell you.[1] So it's useful to know the basic anatomy of search data because it will help you understand what *can* and *can't* be analyzed. We'll cover just the basics here. (See Avi Rappoport's more extensive coverage of the topic at the end of this chapter.)

Minimally, your data consists of records of queries that were submitted to your site's search engine. On a good day, your data will also include the *numbers of results* each query retrieved. On a really good day, each query will be *date/time stamped* so you can get an idea of when different searches were happening. On a really, really good day, your data will also include information on who—such as an individual, by way of tracking her cookie, or a segment of users that you determine by their login credentials—is actually doing the searching.

Here's a tiny sample of query data that must have arrived on one of those really, really good days. It comes from a U.S. state government Web site

---

[1] Once you have the raw data, you'll need to parse out the good stuff, and then use a spreadsheet or application to analyze it. Here's a PERL script from the good people at Michigan State University that you can use to parse it: ₪ www.rosenfeldmedia.com/books/searchanalytics/content/code_samples/. And here's a spreadsheet you can use to analyze it: ₪ http://rosenfeldmedia.com/books/searchanalytics/blog/free_ms_excel_template_for_ana/

that uses Google Search Appliance. It's really ugly stuff; so to make it more readable, we've bolded the critical elements: **IP address, time/date stamp, query**, and **# of results**:

```
XXX.XXX.X.104 - - [10/Jul/2006:10:25:46 -0800] "GET
/search?access=p&entqr=0&output=xml_no_dtd&sort=date%3AD%3AL%3Ad1&ud=1&site=
AllSites&ie=UTF-8&client=www&oe=UTF-
8&proxystylesheet=www&q=lincense+plate&ip=XXX.XXX.X.104 HTTP/1.1" 200 971 0
0.02
XXX.XXX.X.104 - - [10/Jul/2006:10:25:48 -0800] "GET
/search?access=p&entqr=0&output=xml_no_dtd&sort=date%3AD%3AL%3Ad1&ie=UTF-
8&client=www&q=license+plate
&ud=1&site=AllSites&spell=1&oe=UTF-8&proxystylesheet=www&ip=XXX.XXX.X.104
HTTP/1.1" 200 8283 146 0.16
```

Even with a little bit of data—in this case, two queries—we can learn something about how people search a site. In this case, the searcher from IP address ...104 entered lincense plate at 10:25 a.m. on July 10, 2006, and retrieved zero results (that's the next-to-last number in each record). No surprise there. Just a couple seconds later, the searcher entered license plate and retrieved 146 results.

These are just two queries, but they certainly can get you thinking. For example, we might reasonably guess that the first effort was a typo. If, during our analysis, we saw lots more typos, we probably ought to make sure the search engine could handle spellchecking. And we might want to make extra sure that, if license plate was a frequent query, the site contained good content on license plates, and that it always came up at the top of the search results page. There are many more questions and ideas that would come up from reviewing the search data. But most of all, we'd like to know if the users were happy with the experience. In this example, were they?

Heaven knows. The data is good at telling us *what* happened, but it doesn't tell *why* the session ended there. You'll need to use a qualitative research method if you wanted to learn more. (We'll get into this *what/why* dichotomy quite a bit in Chapter 11, "Bridging Web Analytics and User Experience.")

George Kingsley Zipf, Harvard Linguist and Hockey Star

Of course, we've just been looking at a tiny slice of a search log. And as interesting as it is, the true power of SSA comes from collectively analyzing the thousands or millions of such interactions that take place on your site during a given period of time. That's when the patterns emerge, when trends take shape, and when there's enough activity to merit measuring— and drawing interesting conclusions.

Nowhere is the value of statistical analysis more apparent than when viewing the Zipf Distribution, named for Harvard linguist George Kingsley Zipf, who, as you'd expect from a linguist, liked to count words.[2] He found that a few terms were used quite often, while many were hardly used at all. We find the same thing when tallying up queries from most to least frequent, as in Figure 2.4.

The Zipf distribution—which emerges when tallying just about any site's search data—shows that the few most common queries account for a surprisingly large portion of all search activity during any given period. (Remember in Chapter 1, "How Search Site Analytics Can Save Your Butt," how John Ferrara focused exclusively on those common queries.) You can see how tall and narrow what we'll call the "short head" is, and how quickly it drops down to the "long tail" of esoteric queries (technically, described as "twosies" and "onesies"). In fact, we're only showing the first 500 or so queries here; in reality, this site's long tail would extend into the tens of thousands, many meters to the right of where you sit.

---

2 You may not have heard of Zipf, but you've probably heard of the 80/20 Rule, the Pareto Principle, or Power Laws. All relate to the hockey-stick curve's dramatic dropoff from "short head" to long tail.

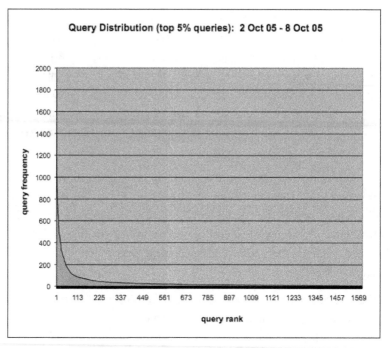

FIGURE 2.4

The hockey-stick-shaped Zipf Distribution shows that a few queries are very popular, while most are not. This example is from Michigan State University, but this distribution is true of just about every Web site and intranet.

It's equally enlightening to examine the same phenomenon when presented textually, as shown in Table 2.1

The most common query, campus map, accounts for 1.4% of all the search activity during this time period. That number, 1.4%, doesn't sound like much, but those top queries add up very quickly—the top 14 most common queries account for 10% of all search activity. (Note to MSU. edu webmaster: better make sure that relevant results come up when users search campus map!)

TABLE 2.1

THE ZIPF DISTRIBUTION SHOWN TEXTUALLY			
Rank	Cumulative %	Count	Query Terms
I	1.40%	7,218	campus map
14	10.53%	2,464	housing
42	20.18%	1,351	webenroll
98	30.01%	650	computer center
221	40.05%	295	msu union
500	50.02%	124	hotels
7,877	80.00%	7	department of surgery

Note how few queries are required to account for 10% of all search activity.
(This data is also from Michigan State University.)

That's incredible—it means that if you invested the small amount of effort needed to ensure that the top 14 queries performed well, you'd improve the search experience for 10% of all users. And if, say, half of your site's users were search dominant,[3] then you've just improved the overall user experience by 5% (10% × 50%). Numbers like this can and should be challenged, and 5% may not sound like much. But 5% here, 3% there... these quickly add up.

It bears noting that we just started with a simple report—presented both visually and as a table—and quickly drew some useful conclusions based on the data presented. That there, folks, is analysis. And that's why reports are only *means,* not *goals.*

And equally important, this analysis scales beautifully. Have the time and resources to go beyond the top 14 queries? No problem—tuning the top 42 queries will get you to the 20% mark. About a 100 gets you to 30%, and so on.

---

3   Usability expert Jakob Nielsen suggests that this is the case; see www.useit.com/alertbox/9707b.html

Ways to Use SSA (and This Book)

So what's the message here? That SSA is an incredibly important tool for helping you understand what users want from your site. And once you have a sense of what they want, you can evaluate and improve all sorts of things that are there to help users get what they want. For instance, you can improve your site as follows:

- **Search system:** SSA will help you understand how people entered searches, where they were when they entered them, and how they interpreted the search results. (We cover this in Chapter 8, "Practical Tips for Improving Search.")

- **Navigation and metadata:** Do certain pages generate a lot more search activity than others? What kinds of searches? And does this suggest that certain navigational options are missing or labeled in a confusing way? SSA will also give you tips on how to shore up your site's navigation and metadata. (We cover this in Chapter 9, "Practical Tips for Improving Site Navigation and Metadata.")

- **Content:** For example, you can study queries that retrieve zero results. Is this because there isn't content on the topic? Should there be? Or is the relevant content mistitled? Or poorly written? SSA will help you determine what content is missing and what to do to existing content to make sure it gets found. (We cover this in Chapter 10, "Practical Tips for Improving Content.")

Whatever design challenges you face, SSA—like any other data analysis—will back up your design decisions with actual facts.

Of course, as much as you'd like to make users happy, you also have to make your employers happy. They have goals—for your organization and for the site itself. (They ought to, at least.) These can be expressed and measured as KPI—Key Performance Indicators. The types of search-related metrics that you saw in Chapter 1 can serve as components to these KPIs—in fact, many organizations that are otherwise sophisticated in their measurement of performance often fall down when it comes to measuring findability. In Chapter 3, we'll help you do what John Ferrara did: use goal-based analysis to measure, monitor, and optimize performance, again and again.

Finally, there are some other important ways to analyze search data:

- **Pattern analysis:** What patterns emerge when you "play" with the data? Can you use those patterns to determine what types of metadata and content are the most important to your searchers? Can you detect changes in seachers' behavior and needs that are seasonal? Do you also find instructive surprises and outliers? (We cover this in Chapter 3, "Pattern Analysis.")

- **Failure analysis:** When searches return no results—or poor results— what can we learn? And what can we do to fix those problems and improve performance? (We cover this in Chapter 4, "Failure Analysis.")

- **Session analysis:** What happens during a specific search session? How do searchers' needs and understanding of the content change as they search? (We cover this in Chapter 5, "Session Analysis.")

- **Audience analysis:** How might we uncover the differences between audience segments and their information needs? And how might we better address those differing needs? (We cover this in Chapter 6, "Audience Analysis.")

What Gets in the Way of SSA?

So you're wondering: if SSA is so valuable, why don't you hear more about it? And why haven't you been taking advantage of it?

There are a few predictable and mostly mundane reasons, such as the following:

- **Lack of awareness:** The idea has been around for years, but so was the Web before it took off. There's simply a lack of critical mass behind SSA getting more attention; hence this book.

- **Technical hurdles:** Your IT people might be too busy to write the scripts to parse your log files or even provide you with access to large and unwieldy data files. This is becoming less of an issue as organizations move toward using analytics applications to access the data; still, you might need a developer's help in writing ad hoc queries.

- **Political hurdles:** Your IT people might be too busy (or instructed *not*) to answer your phone calls. Or they might feel that anything related to search is their and *only* their responsibility (because many equate search with a search engine). There's no simple solution here. Often, your best and only approach will be patience and persistence— just keep trying.

- **Legal hurdles:** Lawyers often freak out any time someone wants access to user data—even if it's for internal use—and issue blanket denials to requests for access. If you can get the attention of your legal department's representative for even 30 seconds, explain to that person that you're interested in analyzing the *collective* behavior of your site's users, rather than digging into the habits of individuals.

- **Lack of data:** Many sites—your personal blog, for example—likely don't generate enough search activity to merit studying. In fact, they probably aren't creating any sort of behavioral stream worth analyzing at all. That said, it's still won't hurt to poke into even a small data set, given that...

- **Lack of tools:** ...the price of analytics tools is coming down. Way down. Like, free, thanks to Google Analytics (though you won't be able to use a hosted service for your intranet). It's not perfect, but it's pretty useful, especially given the price. And if you're working with simple data, Excel will do in a pinch.

But these barriers to taking advantage of SSA don't explain why it's still something of an unknown in most circles. So why has SSA fallen through the cracks?

Who Is Responsible for SSA?

Frankly, in smaller, less advanced organizations, SSA receives little or no attention. It's just one of a few dozen non-urgent aspects of maintaining a Web presence—like meeting accessibility standards or keeping content fresh—that often gets pushed aside as assorted fires get put out. And when it does get done in these settings, it's by a webmaster who already wears nine other hats.

In more advanced settings, where there are entire business units devoted to web analytics and user research, SSA still falls through the cracks. That's because when SSA comes up, it seems just different enough from each unit's existing daily responsibilities to assume that it's someone else's job. Why is that? It comes down to what people are comfortable with, and usually we're comfortable with the familiar.

For example, web analytics people tend to prefer analyzing "cleaner" types of data—like conversion data—that have a more clear impact on the bottom line. (Monitor the Web Analytics Forum Yahoo Group for a week or two, and you'll see what we mean.)[4] The successful conversion of a search is far more difficult to determine, much less measure, as language (and therefore searching) is so ambiguous. So, in a sense, the semantic richness of search query data is a double-edged sword—while the data might be quite interesting, it can be relatively difficult to analyze.

User experience people, on the other hand, tend to be less comfortable with numbers in general and data analysis in particular. They more typically rely upon qualitative analyses, where there are fewer expectations of conclusive, measureable outcomes and more is open to interpretation. And they may assume that analyzing data requires sophisticated expertise in statistical analysis. So, for UX people, SSA is usually on someone else's table.

Let's face it, in most situations today, SSA is no one's job, but it should belong to someone (hence this book). Whatever your perspective—whether you're a web analytics expert, a UX researcher, or a wearer of nine hats—you'll want to have a clear picture of those top most common queries

---

4 http://tech.groups.yahoo.com/group/webanalytics/

and how well your site is performing. And you'll want to have that clear picture this month, next month, next season, and next year. Seeing SSA as part of your *ongoing work* (for example, 5% of your normal week) rather than as a *one-off project* (for example, a 12-hour assignment) will enable you to continually improve your site and make sure that it keeps up with the changes in its environment. The world around it changes, and like a living organism, your site must change as well in order to survive and thrive. And don't lose sleep over when during the process—research, design, development, or maintenance—you tackle SSA. You'll glean something small—good things at each point, none of which will likely take you off on a radical tangent.

Finally, if you're one of those wearers of many hats, don't fret: as mentioned earlier, SSA scales wonderfully. Even if you spend 15 minutes per month looking over the simplest reports—the most frequent queries list and the null results query list—you'll get *something* useful out of your analysis. This month's 15 minutes of tuning can gently grow to 30 minutes next month, and so on. The work is the same—it will fill whatever time you can make or justify for it.

Your Secret Weapon

Thank your lucky stars: SSA remains safely under the radar. No one owns it, and the people in most organizations who are closest to it—the IT folks who manage the search engine—aren't likely to worry much about things like *user intent*. So if you can crack open the data, you (and your organization) will own the keys to a very powerful secret weapon. Read ahead.

Anatomy of a Search Log Entry

Avi Rappoport, Search Tools Consulting—http://searchtools.com/

Though most of us are now using analytics applications that provide some SSA reporting functionality, you may be in a situation where you'll have to create your own reports— either because the analytics application doesn't support your specific needs—or because you don't have access to an analytics application. In both cases, you'll need to process the data yourself.

Working with search engine transaction logs, you'll find the search query, any search parameters (such as language or date), and the number of matches retrieved by the search engine. Most also contain the date and time, and some kind of searcher identifier. Understanding the format makes it easier to understand search analytics reports, recognize what they can and can't tell you, and perform special processing for unusual questions.

Many search engines conform to the NCSA extended Web server log format,[5] so that's what we'll cover here. These text files have a standard field order, with spaces between them. To indicate a field with internal spaces, it needs double quotes or square brackets at the start and end.

However, there's no place in the NCSA extended format for the hit count (the number of items matched in the search), so search engines tend to slide it in the middle or hang it off the end. If your search log format is not documented, you may need to do some sleuthing: you can figure this out by entering several unique searches that you know will generate no matches, and then look in the search log for those terms.

BASIC FIELDS

A simple query entry in this log format looks like this:

```
XX.XX.XX.14 - - [10/Jul/2010:10:24:13 -0800] "GET /search?q=noise HTTP/1.1" 200
    9429 111
```

---

5   The NCSA combined/extended log format is documented at http://publib.boulder.ibm.com/tividd/
    td/ITWSA/ITWSA_info45/en_US/HTML/guide/c-logs.html#combined and http://httpd.
    apache.org/docs/2.2/mod/mod_log_config.html#examples

continues on next page

Anatomy of a Search Log Entry (continued)

We can break that down into fields for better analysis, as shown in Table 2.2.

TABLE 2.2

FIELDS BY POSITION								
	#1	#2	#3	#4	#5	#6	#7	#8
meaning	ip	-	-	date/timestamp	search request	response code	bytes	hits
example	xx.xx.xx.14	-	-	[10/Jul/ 2010:10:24:13 -0800]	"GET /search?q= noise HTTP/1.1"	200	9429	111

Table 2.3 provides even more detail on each field.

WHAT EXTENDED LOG ENTRIES LOOK LIKE

Optional fields can be quite helpful as well. These include the "referer" field (it should be "referrer," but the spec spelled it wrong, so now we're stuck with this misspelling), which can offer insights into site navigation problems; the user-agent for recognizing various platforms using the search; and an optional cookie, which is better than IP address for tracking searchers. To conform to other Web log formats, these fields might come before the *hit count* and *time taken* fields.

An extended log entry could look like this (detailed below in Table 2.4):

```
XX.XX.XX.14 - - [10/Jul/2010:10:24:13 -0800] "GET /search?q=noise HTTP/1.1" 200
9429 111 0028 "http://search.example.com/search?q=sound HTTP/1.1" "Mozilla/5.0
(iPhone; U; CPU iPhone OS 2_2 like Mac OS X; en-us) AppleWebKit/525.18.1
(KHTML, like Gecko) Version/3.1.1 Mobile/5G77 Safari/525.20"
"USERID=CustomerACooke;IMPID=01234"
```

Anatomy of a Search Log Entry (continued)

TABLE 2.3

DETAILS ABOUT FIELDS

Position	Field	Example	Meaning
#1	IP or host name	XX.XX.XX.14	ID of the computer sending the search.
#2	auth. user	-	usually empty, RFC931 authentication
#3	user name	-	usually empty
#4a	date	[10/Jul/2010	date of the query in standard form
#4b	time	:10:24:13	time of the query in standard form
#4c	offset	-0800]	offset time from GMT *
#5a	request	"GET	HTTP results (form action)
#5b	URL	/search.html	search results page URL
#5c	parameters	?query=noise	search terms and other options
#5d	version	HTTP/1.1"	version (always the same)
#6	response code	200	server response code (if it's not 200, you are in trouble)
#7	bytes	9249	bytes returned (the size of the search results HTML page)
#8 (non-standard but widely used)	hit count	111	number of matches found**

* The GMT offset is important because you must have accurate timestamps to look for patterns of usage, such as spikes of traffic at lunchtime. Tracking the time relative to GMT lets analytics systems merge search logs from multiple time zones, which is especially important when adjusting for Daylight Savings Time.

** Some search engines return the approximate number of hits, rather than provide a definitive number. This is usually because they are reserving the option to check whether the user has security access to additional documents. If you don't have confidential documents, you may be able to disable the access check and get a real number.

continues on next page

Anatomy of a Search Log Entry (continued)

TABLE 2.4

EXTENDED FIELDS			
Position	Field	Example	Meaning
#9	referer URL	http://search.example.com/search?q=sound	The page that the user was on when he searched: in this case, from a search results page for the query "sound".
#10	user-agent	"Mozilla/5.0 (iPhone; U; CPU iPhone OS 2_2 like Mac OS...	The browser or app that sent the query. These are most useful for getting client metrics (especially mobile) and recognizing robot crawlers.
#11	cookie	"USERID=CustomerA; IMPID=01234"	Cookie for server session (rare).

SEARCH PARAMETERS

Most search engines stick to the common format for additional options and settings (such as language or in the search part of the request). They start after the results page URL with a question mark and then put in a code followed by an equal sign followed by a value, delimited by an ampersand (or comma or semicolon), like this:

```
search.html?qq=noise&zone=all
```

There's no standard, so the query parameter might be q, qq, qt, qry, query, w, words, s, st, search, or something else entirely. This, and all the other codes, should be documented by the search vendor or open-source group. (We've provided an example below, as well as details in Table 2.5.) You'll find this information useful if you need to "teach" your analytics application what to look for to identify—and parse out—actual queries from your logs. Here is an example of a query parameter:

```
search?q=noise&l=f1&s=21&p=20v=housewares&i=1
```

Anatomy of a Search Log Entry (continued)

TABLE 2.5

QUERY PARAMETERS			
Code	Field	Example	Meaning
q	query	q=noise	The search terms, in this case "noise"
l	language	l=fi	The searcher's language, here it's Finnish
s	start	s=21	Start the display at result number 21
p	per page	p=20	Show 20 results per page
v	section	v=housewares	Limit the query to the housewares section
i	simple	i=1	Show the simple search interface

The contents of the log file enable site search analytics: the entries provide the evidence needed to deduce how your users are searching and how well the site search is helping them. Cherish the logs or at least keep an archive: you may need to go back someday.

Summary

- SSA offers a unique treasure trove of data worth tapping because it's the one place where users tell you *in their own words* what they want from your site.

- SSA provides different information about users than insights you normally get from SEM (Search Engine Marketing) and SEO (Search Engine Optimization). Think of people searching the Web as people you want to attract to your site, while people searching your site are customers you want to retain. SSA is concerned with the latter.

- Query data can be captured in search engine logs or by analytics applications that harvest information on users' actions on your site.

- When users search your site, they typically will have more specific needs (and queries) than when they search for information on the Web.

- As the Zipf distribution shows, a little SSA goes a long way. Start by improving the performance of your site's most common queries; they will account for a huge portion of your search activity.

- Use pattern analysis, session analysis, failure analysis, and audience analysis to analyze your query data, diagnose problems, and determine ways to improve your site's content, navigation, and search system.

- Use goal-based analysis to determine new ways to measure your site's performance and connect search to your organization's KPI (Key Performance Indicators).

CHAPTER 3

Pattern Analysis

Analysis as a Form of Play   34
Getting Started with Pattern Analysis   36
Patterns to Consider   40
Finding Patterns in the Long Tail   52
Anti-Pattern Analysis: Surprises and Outliers   55
Summary   60

The next five chapters (including this one) cover various ways to analyze and derive new insights from your query data that can directly improve your site's user experience. We'll start by looking at the patterns and oddities that emerge from your data if you play with it (and stare at it long enough).

Analysis as a Form of Play

In pattern analysis, we look for what our queries have in common: tone, length, topic, type, and more. We also explore what's odd—are there queries that don't fit with the rest? We then study those groups and misfits to see if we can learn something new about our searchers and the content they want and need. Does their language match the tone of our content? Are they requesting certain types of content more than others? Do searchers demonstrate certain kinds of information needs at particular times of the year? Or day?

How does pattern analysis work? We simply play with our data and see what emerges. Yes, it's essentially that simple: we play. And it's as fun as it sounds.

The Simple Part

The simple part about pattern analysis is that as humans we're naturally built to detect patterns, especially semantic ones. Don't believe me? Well, take a quick look at this list of words in Table 3.1.

TABLE 3.1

GOOGLE COMMON QUERIES			
#1	indiana earthquake	#11	earthquakes today
#2	isabelle caro photos	#12	laura govan
#3	candace cameron bure	#13	moshe katsav
#4	lily shang	#14	indystar
#5	amazon eve	#15	happy new years
#6	isabelle caro before anorexia	#16	new year quotes funny
#7	new years eve 2011	#17	brie larson
#8	billy taylor	#18	christine o donnell
#9	jamie foxx	#19	billy boyd
#10	2011 predictions	#20	feliz ano nuevo

A set of common queries logged by Google Trends, December 30, 2010.

What did you notice? Any patterns emerge? Any outliers?

You may have noticed many queries that were people's names (for example, laura govan and billy taylor), while others were related to the end of the year (new year quotes funny and 2011 predictions), and the rest were an odd mix of stuff pertaining to mostly earthquakes.

Or you might have divided the people into different categories (for example, politicians, musicians, comedians) or by gender. You might have sussed out some geographic issues, such as queries that have some regional or local significance (for example, former Israeli president moshe katsav and indiana earthquake). Or something else completely different.

Whatever patterns emerged for you, you probably performed some or all of these four pattern analysis tasks without even realizing it:

- You *sampled* the content to get a sense of what was there.

- You *grouped* things that seemed to go together.

- You may have *sorted* them to get a different collective look at them.

- And you likely *iterated* your way through a few passes at them before you were satisfied with what you came up with.

If you're not sure how to begin pattern analysis, try these four tasks and let your mind wander through the data. And remember, no single pattern is the "right" one!

The Fun Part

When I teach workshops on site search analytics, I have my students do a hands-on pattern analysis exercise. Even though I intentionally provide minimal instructions, it's amazing how quickly they become absorbed in the process of detecting patterns and categorizing queries. (And no, my students aren't exclusively data modelers, librarians, or other data nerds.) They arrive at conclusions that aren't the same—their groups overlap, their interpretations differ—and they greatly enjoy comparing their results. Some revel in their differences; others are, frankly, a little uncomfortable with the lack of a "correct" set of patterns. That's the precise moment at which I recommend that they consider following up their pattern analysis with a more qualitative technique, like card sorting, to determine the most common, if not "correct," groupings.

Some of my students are skeptical of the idea of "playing" with the data. They feel they should be engaging in more serious statistical analysis. Yet many statisticians will tell you that you should perform what they call "Exploratory Data Analysis"*before* you tackle formal statistical testing.[1] Until you first have a sense of the data—and its patterns—you might not have a good idea of which statistical tests you should be applying.

So let's have some fun.

Getting Started with Pattern Analysis

Good news: you already have the tools—your brain included—necessary for pattern analysis. I'll wager that you already own a copy of Microsoft Excel; if not, you could certainly create a spreadsheet in a free tool like Google Documents or OpenOffice. To get started, you'll need some minimal data: queries (at least from the short head) and how frequently they were searched on your site. You might grab these by exporting them from your analytics application or by using this PERL script ▟ www.rosenfeldmedia.com/books/downloads/searchanalytics/loganalyzer.txt to parse them from your server log.

Next, create two columns in your spreadsheet—one for your unique queries, the other for their frequency counts—and import or paste in your data. If you know the date range for your data sample, mention it in the spreadsheet so you won't forget it later. Here's an example of such a spreadsheet that contains common queries from Michigan State University's Web site in Figure 3.1. We'll return to the MSU example throughout this chapter.

---

[1] See Wikipedia for more on Exploratory Data Analysis: http://en.wikipedia.org/wiki/Exploratory_data_analysis

Count	Unique Query
2747	stuinfo
768	deans list
672	registrar
595	dean's list
557	mail
509	schedule of courses
454	spartantrak
434	bookstore
409	email
401	student info
396	human resources
391	im west
375	study abroad
360	campus map
359	computer store
357	housing
355	transcripts
346	jobs
345	map
325	library
314	enrollment
309	enroll
305	cemscores
298	degree navigator
297	transfer credits
295	olin
288	angel
286	honors college
282	tuition
275	stu info
244	transfer
243	financial aid
240	employment
237	spartan trak
235	academic calendar
232	parking
221	webenroll
210	hr
207	calendar

FIGURE 3.1

A week's worth of Michigan State University queries, sorted by frequency.

I've created a souped-up version of this spreadsheet (shown in Figure 3.2), which I encourage you to download and use as a template. (You can get it here: ᛗ http://rosenfeldmedia.com/books/searchanalytics/blog/free_ms_excel_template_for_ana/.) Here's what the spreadsheet contains:

- **Rank:** Each query's rank in terms of frequency.

- **Percent:** The percentage of overall search activity that each unique query is responsible for (out of all your site's search activity).

Michigan State University--Individual Queries
7 May 06 - 13 May 06
http://search.msu.edu/index.php?q=

90,254	Total Queries in Sample
32,000	Total Unique Queries in Sample
2.82	Average # Times Unique Queries were Performed
1.00	Median # Times Unique Queries were Performed
2.35	Average # Terms/Unique Query
16.28	Average # Characters/Unique Query

Rank	Percent	Cumulative Percent	Count	Unique Query	Link
1	3.0436	3.0436	2747	stuinfo	search
2	0.8509	3.8946	768	deans list	search
3	0.7446	4.6391	672	registrar	search
4	0.6593	5.2984	595	dean's list	search
5	0.6171	5.9155	557	mail	search
6	0.5640	6.4795	509	schedule of courses	search
7	0.5030	6.9825	454	spartantrak	search
8	0.4809	7.4634	434	bookstore	search
9	0.4532	7.9165	409	email	search
10	0.4443	8.3608	401	student info	search
11	0.4388	8.7996	396	human resources	search
12	0.4332	9.2328	391	im west	search
13	0.4155	9.6483	375	study abroad	search
14	0.3989	10.0472	360	campus map	search
15	0.3978	10.4450	359	computer store	search
16	0.3956	10.8405	357	housing	search
17	0.3933	11.2339	355	transcripts	search
18	0.3834	11.6172	346	jobs	search
19	0.3823	11.9995	345	map	search
20	0.3601	12.3596	325	library	search
21	0.3479	12.7075	314	enrollment	search
22	0.3424	13.0498	309	enroll	search
23	0.3379	13.3878	305	cemscores	search
24	0.3302	13.7180	298	degree navigator	search
25	0.3291	14.0470	297	transfer credits	search

FIGURE 3.2

The same data as in Figure 3.1—now all gussied-up.

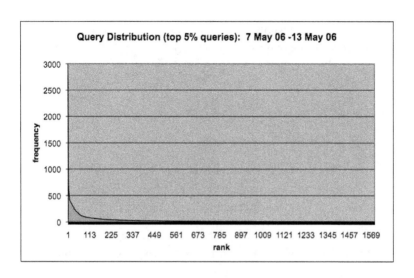

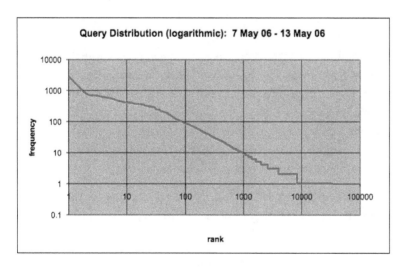

- **Cumulative Percent:** The percentages of all the queries added up. If you're looking at query #3 (registrar), the Cumulative Percent shows the sum of the first three queries' percentages (4.6391 = 3.0436 + 0.8509 + 0.7446).

- **Count:** How often each unique query was searched.

- **Unique Query:** The query itself.

- **Link:** I've done a little fancy programming to provide a live link to execute each unique query on the Michigan State Web site. This just makes it easier to test each query.

- I've also provided some other information at the top—such as the average number of terms per query— as a pair of fancy Zipf distributions to help you visualize the data.

Patterns to Consider

Now go ahead and take a deeper look at and start playing with the MSU queries. Stare at them for a bit, scan up and down a bit, and then stare again. Do you detect anything interesting, or surprising, about the language searchers are using in their queries? Were you surprised that stuinfo is used more frequently than stu info? Or that map was as high (or low) as it was? Did you happen to notice lots of queries that seemed to deal with places on campus and others that seemed to be about courses?

With each new pass at the data, you'll come up with more questions. Following are some of the types of patterns you might encounter when analyzing your own query data.

To use this spreadsheet for your own analysis, paste your queries and query count data into the *Unique Query* and *Count* columns, respectively. You may need to select both columns and sort *Count* from largest to smallest in order to have your queries sorted by frequency (if they're not already). The other columns should automatically be calculated and filled, and you should be ready to move forward with finding and analyzing patterns.

Tonal Patterns

Notice the tone or flavor of these terms. Do you see jargon (for example, spartantrak and cemscores)? Abbreviations (such as im west and hr)? Most importantly, does this language match what you expected?

This is one of those *so-obvious-that-it's-not* questions to ask.

For example, I consulted for a large U.S. government agency that's dedicated to serving health professionals. It found that there were many more instances of queries that were apparently coming from laymen (who would search for swine flu) than there were from its core audience of doctors, nurses, and health-care researchers (who would search for h1n1). This resulted in a major rethinking of the site's mission. ("Hmmm, maybe we ought to also serve everyday Joes who are worried that their kids might be coming down with something serious.") Accordingly, the agency drastically changed its content's tone and its tagging to meet those unanticipated needs.

As you start to get a sense of the language of your site's searchers, consider the language of your site's content. Are there obvious differences? If you're the Michigan State University webmaster, you may be surprised to find that searchers tend to abbreviate more frequently than you'd expect. For example, they may use the term im west rather than West Intramural Sports Building. So you might want to give your content authors a list of commonplace name abbreviations to use when tagging relevant pages.

Synonym Patterns

Synonyms are also instructive when it comes to understanding the tone of voice that your searchers are likely to take, as well as the tone your content ought to take. So let's do a little bit of analysis of our common queries to determine potential synonyms, continuing with our Michigan State University example.

In the following spreadsheet, I took MSU's 50 most frequent unique queries (if I had more time, I'd have used more) and their percentages (to remind you, these are percentages of overall search activity that each unique query accounted for). I did this simply by copying and pasting them from the previous spreadsheet in Figure 3.2.

I then looked for queries among them that seemed synonymous (such as jobs and employment) and grouped them. Finally, for each cluster, I tallied up the individual queries' percentages to determine a cumulative percentage for that cluster (see Figure 3.3).

Metadata values

Query	Cumulative Percentage	Query	Cumulative Percentage
stuinfo	3.04%	jobs	0.38%
student info	0.44%	employment	0.27%
stu info	0.30%	**cluster total**	**0.65%**
cluster total	**3.79%**	library	**0.36%**
deans list	0.85%	enrollment	0.35%
dean's list	0.56%	enroll	0.34%
cluster total	**1.51%**	webenroll	0.24%
registrar	**0.74%**	web enroll	0.23%
mail	0.62%	**cluster total**	**1.52%**
email	0.45%	cemscores	**0.34%**
cluster total	**1.81%**	degree navigator	**0.33%**
schedule of courses	**0.56%**	transfer credits	**0.33%**
spartantrak	0.50%	olin	**0.33%**
spartan trak	0.26%	angel	**0.32%**
cluster total	**1.33%**	honors college	**0.32%**
bookstore	0.48%	tuition	**0.31%**
stores	0.21%	transfer	**0.27%**
bookstores	0.21%	financial aid	**0.27%**
computer store	0.40%	academic calendar	0.26%
cluster total	**1.31%**	calendar	0.23%
human resources	0.44%	**cluster total**	**0.49%**
HR	0.23%	parking	0.26%
cluster total	**0.67%**	payroll	**0.22%**
im west	**0.43%**	dpps	**0.22%**
study abroad	**0.42%**	state news	**0.22%**
campus map	0.40%	grades	**0.21%**
map	0.38%	nursing	**0.21%**
cluster total	**1.63%**	psychology	**0.21%**
housing	**0.40%**	college of education	**0.20%**
transcripts	0.39%		
transcript	0.20%		
cluster total	**0.99%**		

FIGURE 3.3

Clusters of synonymous queries and their respective percentages of search traffic over a given time period.

The whole exercise took less than an hour.

The first cluster of synonymous terms is related to student information (stuinfo, student info, and stu info) and comprises about 3.8% of all the searches that week. Of those three variants, we can tell that stuinfo is by far more common than its synonymous siblings, accounting for about 3% of that week's searches alone. (This isn't surprising, because at Michigan State University, stuinfo happens to be the official name of a branded application.)

Knowing that one term is far more common than others is useful if you're responsible for your site's information architecture. For example, if you're creating a set of metadata (for example, a thesaurus), you may need to determine "preferred terms," variants that are selected as the most appropriate to use. So you might guess that stuinfo is, at least according to searchers, the best variant to choose to tag documents related to student information.

It's also handy to know a preferred term when you're coming up with a document's title. And if you are developing a site-wide taxonomy, you can typically include only a single, preferred term—and now you know that stuinfo is probably the best one.

Even if you don't need to determine a single preferred term, you now have a sense of the terms that are most likely to resonate with users. This can be pretty useful to share with your site's content authors and can influence their editorial policy. After all, now they have data to help them make—or validate—their decisions on usage.

And perhaps most importantly, you now will have a sense of the richness of searchers' language.

Time-Based Patterns

Pattern hunting can get especially interesting when you introduce the element of time into your analysis. After all, your searchers' information needs are constantly changing, as is your content. SSA can tell you what's important and when, and you can tune your site—and your content strategy—accordingly.[2]

You might consider analyzing query patterns by such finely grained time segments as hours. For example, you might find that your intranet experiences a high level of queries for calendar, meetings, and events as the workday begins; menu as stomachs rumble during the lunch hour's approach; and weather and traffic as the day ends and thoughts turn to the commute home. Why not cycle these various kinds of content on your home page based on the time of day?

---

2   Every organization has decided of late that it needs a "content strategy," and this is a good thing. Consult Kristina Halvorson's book *Content Strategy for the Web* as a good starting place.

Tuning Search for Phrase Queries

Walter Underwood, Lead Engineer, MarkLogic Corporation

Phrase queries may be more common than you would expect from looking at the top queries. In fact, it's common for more than half of all query traffic to be phrases.

To get good relevance for phrase queries (queries with more than one word), you will probably need to do additional search engine tuning. This tuning pays off when your CEO searches for his own name and sees his bio as the first hit.

Most phrase queries are either proper nouns or common noun phrases. A proper noun phrase is a specific person, place, or thing: Maurice Duruflé, United Way, Rice University Bookstore, or Wings of Desire. Other noun phrases act like common nouns: French composer, charitable contribution, campus store, or foreign film.

Noun phrases may show a lot of vocabulary variation, because individuals choose different words with similar meanings. A searcher might choose charitable or charity and combine that with contribution or donation. Now we have four phrase queries used to search for the same thing. These four are different ways of expressing the same information need as a query:

- charitable contribution

- charitable donation

- charity contribution

- charity donation

With query counts spread between these variants, the most common one might be far down your list of most frequent queries. If you add the counts together, you will get a more accurate picture of the importance of this information need. For example, if charitable contribution showed up 100

Tuning Search for Phrase Queries (continued)

times and the others 50, 25, and 25, then the true frequency for this question would be 200 (or more), not 100. The variation in vocabulary spreads the concept over many different query phrases.

Your search engine might convert charitable to the root word charity with an English stemmer, but it is unlikely to treat donation and contribution as the same word. You can add donation and contribution to the synonyms used by your search engine and then re-index to treat them the same.

A "stemmer" converts words to their base forms, plural to singular, past tense to present, and so on. You can check the behavior of your stemmer by creating two test documents, each containing one word, either charity or charitable. Submit those to your search engine and then use those two words individually as queries to see if both documents match equally. If they don't match, then you can make those two words synonyms.

Proper noun queries will usually be entered the same by all searchers, with little or no variation in vocabulary. It is extremely unlikely that someone searching for Steve Jobs would type steve careers. Proper noun queries behave more like single words, so they will benefit from spelling correction or "fuzzy search," but rarely need synonyms.

You may see spacing variants in phrase queries. Is it Ghost Busters or Ghostbusters? Is it web site or website? There might not even be an official correct spelling. Sony Pictures prefers Ghostbusters, but the movie's title sequence splits it into two words. The AP Stylebook started allowing "website" in April 2010, so articles published before then correctly use "Web site." Hyphenation may be involved, too—is it Spiderman, Spider Man, or Spider-Man? Even when there is a clearly correct choice, your searchers may split or join the words creatively, searching for bat man or spaceghost. Most search applications will encounter a limited set of these sorts of terms, so synonyms are an effective way to handle them.

MICHIGAN STATE
UNIVERSITY

Search Analysis -- www.msu.edu -- Seasonality --
Richard Wiggins -- wiggins@msu.edu

Sep 05 #	query	Oct 05 #	query	Nov 05 #	query	Dec 05 #	query	Jan 06 #	query	Feb 06 #	query	Mar 06 #
1363	angel	1793	cse 101	2058	cse 101	1447	cse 101	1400	bookstore	1184	capa	618
1357	capa	1180	capa	797	capa	845	capa	842	bookstores	1030	lon capa	443
1251	lon capa	1017	lon capa	642	angel	799	library	809	calendar	840	study abroad	428
1215	cse 101	689	angel	599	cse101	729	lon capa	688	campus map	823	angel	411
1058	football	872	football	593	study abroad	696	angel	599	schedule of courses	664	lon-capa	391
834	campus map	774	study abroad	592	lon capa	675	bookstore	578	map	656	library	352
781	map	743	career gallery	571	library	629	math	574	academic calendar	584	olin	333
680	study abroad	722	map	532	football	626	cemscores	552	study abroad	543	campus map	321
625	lon-capa	664	spartan rak	519	olin	600	cata	497	housing	530	spartant rak	318
586	im west	656	career fair	506	campus map	599	campus map	483	registrar	506	cata	311
576	library	650	library	496	map	576	study abroad	481	stuinfo	477	housing	290
510	computer store	583	campus map	450	housing	568	map	413	human resources	467	map	280
504	spartan rak	532	lon-capa	388	spartant rak	538	olin	396	sbs	462	im west	279
484	football schedule	502	wharton center	379	cemscores	506	housing	364	im west	409	computer store	275
							chemistr		spartant		state	

FIGURE 3.4
Notice the monthly change in Michigan State University searchers' needs.

Of course, you might not have the opportunity—or the need—to cycle your content on a daily basis. But it is highly likely that there is at least a seasonality to your site's information usage, and longitudinal pattern analysis will help you expose and address it. Our colleague Rich Wiggins did just that at Michigan State University; building on the kind of categorization exercise described earlier, Rich analyzed an entire year's worth of data (well, not quite, he reviewed one week per month). He color-coded his categories, and the result is the visually instructive table in Figure 3.4.

Apr 06 query	#	May 06 query	#	Jun 06 query	#	Jul 06 query	#	Aug 06 query	#	Sep 06 query	#
library	1390	library	2747	stuinfo	750	housing	613	stuinfo	1157	football	1408
angel	897	angel	768	deans list	583	library	395	housing	858	library	1304
email	868	schedule of courses	672	registrar	447	map	393	bookstore	703	im west	1160
im west	715	campus map	595	dean's list	439	campus map	379	map	567	campus map	1034
basketball	693	study abroad	557	mail	394	stuinfo	359	campus map	566	angel	1007
human resources	627	map	509	schedule of courses	392	computer store	348	human resources	553	map	932
tuition	620	olin	454	spartant rak	378	human resources	343	computer store	553	football schedule	855
transcripts	575	rha	434	bookstore	354	schedule of courses	295	library	463	study abroad	641
study abroad	541	housing	409	email	347	registrar	295	registrar	454	computer store	547
registrar	530	honors college	401	student info	330	im west	287	study abroad	426	stuinfo	532
mail	523	stuinfo	396	human resources	290	study abroad	282	jobs	417	olin	525
stuinfo	490	registrar	391	im west	278	academic calendar	260	schedule of courses	415	cata	512
housing	472	cata	375	study abroad	275	calendar	242	football	397	spartant rak	492
jobs	429	campus map	360	transcripts	274	email	240	spartant rak	390	lon capa	490
spartant		human resourc		compute		schedule of					

Queries regarding finding one's way around campus (coded black) spike in September and January, as each semester begins, as do the beige-colored queries for the bookstore and athletics. Conversely, searchers for the library (orange) spike as term papers come due. Michigan State can use this data to determine what should go where and when. For example, it might make the football team's schedule (and a way to purchase football tickets) quite prominent on the site's main page as the season approaches. Toward each semester's end, MSU could feature the times its libraries open and close.

When you do your own analysis, don't just look for seasonal patterns; different rhythms apply in different contexts. Retailers, for example, may find that customers search for varying products depending on the time of day. Searches of a customer support knowledge base may reveal that weekday searches relate to a company's business-class products, while the weekend's searches are for its consumer-facing products.

Time and time again (excuse the pun), I've found organizations to be surprised at the role time plays in shaping their searchers' information needs. And they are overjoyed at the opportunities that are opened up to them; now they have the data they need to inform their editorial agenda in a narrow sense and, more broadly, their overall content strategy.

Question Patterns

If you want to dig even deeper into understanding the nature of the information needs behind your searchers' queries (and who doesn't?), try hunting for patterns that seem to describe common *question types* that searchers seem to be asking. In other words, by analyzing queries you can categorize the gaps in your searchers' knowledge.

Let's return to our Michigan State University example. In the spreadsheet in Figure 3.5, I've taken the queries and query clusters from Figure 3.3, as well as their respective percentages of all search traffic. (Remember, these are only the top 50 short head queries.)

Then I did something very subjective: for each query or query cluster, I tried to categorize the kind of question or need the query represented. So when students searched for transcripts or transcript, I inferred that they were wondering how to get a copy of their academic transcript (complete a desired task). Or, perhaps, they were wondering which of the university's *services* would help them accomplish this task. (In this case, it's the Office of the Registrar.) I've noted four potential information needs in the columns I've added to the right: *place, department/program, service,* and *task.*

Query Cluster	Cumulative Percentage	Potential Metadata Attributes			
		Place	Dep't/ Program	Service	Task
stuinfo, student info, stu info	3.79%				■
mail, email	1.81%				■
campus map, map	1.63%				■
enrollment, enroll, webenroll, web enroll	1.52%				■
deans list, dean's list	1.51%				
spartantrak, spartan trak	1.33%				
bookstore, stores, bookstores, computer store	1.31%	■			■
transcripts, transcript	0.99%				■
registrar	0.74%		■		
human resources, HR	0.67%				
jobs, employment	0.65%				■
schedule of courses	0.56%				
academic calendar, calendar	0.49%				
im west	0.43%	■	■		
study abroad	0.42%		■		
housing	0.40%	■	■		
library	0.36%	■	■		
cemscores	0.34%				
degree navigator	0.33%				
transfer credits	0.33%				
olin	0.33%	■			
angel	0.32%				
honors college	0.32%		■		
tuition	0.31%				■
transfer	0.27%				
financial aid	0.27%	■	■		■
parking	0.26%	■	■		
payroll	0.22%				
dpps	0.22%				
state news	0.22%				■
grades	0.21%		■		■
nursing	0.21%		■		
psychology	0.21%		■		
college of education	0.20%		■		
Percentage of Queries by Metadata Attribute		4.01%	5.14%	12.99%	11.40%

FIGURE 3.5
I've come with four ways to categorize queries and query clusters: place, department/program, service, and task. Some queries and query clusters fit in multiple categories. For example, the query cluster of transcripts/transcript is an instance of both a task and a service.

How did I arrive at these categories? After I started to review and contextualize the first few queries and query clusters, *service* and *task* seemed to make sense right away. As I continued my analysis, *place, department,* and *program* emerged. Once these new categories surfaced, I had to add new columns and return to the first few query clusters and terms to see if these new categories would describe them as well. Later, I found that *department* and *program* were quite similar, and decided to merge them into a single attribute.

After I completed the process of categorizing and classifying each query and query cluster, I totaled the percentages of queries associated with each attribute. For example, to arrive at "place's" 4.01% score, I added the percentages associated with bookstore, stores, bookstores, computer store, im west, library, and other queries in that category. Or, put another way, I simply added up all the "x's" in that column. Now I have a sense of which categories are most represented among the site's search traffic. Queries dealing with *services* (%12.99) and *tasks* (%11.40) are more common than those associated with *places* (4.01%) and *departments/ programs* (5.14%).

So what does this analysis tell us?

We now have at least a partial understanding of the kinds of information needs this particular group of searchers has. And thanks to tallying up their respective percentages, we can prioritize those categories. As with card-sorting exercises, we can use these categories to inform a site-wide hierarchy. Or we can use the categories to help us make decisions about which metadata types to invest in—we have a sense that there are four decent candidates, and if we can't afford to create and apply them all at once, we know which ones should "go first."

The analysis would certainly be better if I had used more queries—again, these are based on just the top 50. And it would be even better if I'd had multiple people do this exercise, not just your humble author. But even a single pass at the data—in the directed way I've just described—will force you to delve more deeply into understanding your searchers' information needs.

Answer Patterns

In the last section, we tried to deduce the questions—or information needs—that searchers have. How about doing the same thing for the *answers* they hope to receive?

We can repeat the same type of exercise, using the exact same data, but this time, let's look for patterns that describe the kinds of answers—in terms of *content types*—that searchers may hope to find.

To determine possible content types, review your common queries and query clusters, but this time ask a different question: "What *kind* of content would searchers want when they searched this term?" In the spreadsheet in Figure 3.6 (on the following page), I'm using the same Michigan State University queries and query clusters, and their respective percentages of search traffic. But the columns to the right show the kinds of content types I thought each query was intended to retrieve.

Here I've identified six reasonable content types:

- **Applications** (Such as a piece of software which has a unique function and its own interface, such as a system for accessing one's grades)

- **News and Announcements** (For example, press releases)

- **Navigation pages** (For subsites—often, searchers just want to go straight to a site for a department or other program)

- **Reference pages** (Such as the Dean's List or a list of campus cafeterias)

- **Contact info pages** (Records from a directory or subsites' "about us" pages)

- **Instructions** (For example, how to make an appointment for a physical exam or how to use the email system)

As in the last section, queries and query clusters can be included within more than one category. And, as before, the percentages of queries per content type will help you prioritize these six content types. *Application* and *reference pages* are clearly the types of content that most searchers are looking for here.

So how will this help you?

If you're responsible for your organization's document management or content management system, you might find it useful to have a strong sense of what types of content formats are connected to common queries. That will help you make better decisions about which content types to address first in a content migration plan. And if you are tasked with

Query Cluster	Cumulative Percentage	application
stuinfo, student info, stu info	3.79%	
mail, email	1.81%	
campus map, map	1.63%	
enrollment, enroll, webenroll, web enroll	1.52%	
deans list, dean's list	1.51%	
spartantrak, spartan trak	1.33%	
bookstore, stores, bookstores, computer store	1.31%	
transcripts, transcript	0.99%	
registrar	0.74%	
human resources, HR	0.67%	
jobs, employment	0.65%	
schedule of courses	0.56%	
academic calendar, calendar	0.49%	
im west	0.43%	
study abroad	0.42%	
housing	0.40%	
library	0.36%	
cemscores	0.34%	
degree navigator	0.33%	
transfer credits	0.33%	
olin	0.33%	
angel	0.32%	
honors college	0.32%	
tuition	0.31%	
transfer	0.27%	
financial aid	0.27%	
parking	0.26%	
payroll	0.22%	
dpps	0.22%	
state news	0.22%	
grades	0.21%	
nursing	0.21%	
psychology	0.21%	
college of education	0.20%	
	11.77%	

FIGURE 3.6 Determining content types from the bottom up and matching them to queries and query clusters.

developing *schema* for specific kinds of content, or a unique set of templates to fit your site's content, you now have a decent idea of which ones to create and where to start. Finally, if you have your query data segmented appropriately, you can do this same analysis for specific audiences to learn which types of content are especially important to them.

Finding Patterns in the Long Tail

So far I've advised you to focus on the short head in your pattern analysis. I know you'll learn more as you iterate over the data, and I recommend that you scale up the number of unique queries you analyze as time and resources permit.

Candidate Content Types				
news/ announcement	navigation page	reference	contact info	instructions
4.27%	5.91%	10.50%	5.79%	8.60%

A few organizations are so SSA-gung ho that they have maximized most of the analytical opportunities afforded by the short head and have moved on to the long tail. If you get to that point—and many congratulations if you do—you'll be happy to know that you'll analyze the data in much the same way I've shown you so far. The exception is that you'll want to start with a random sample of 100 or perhaps 50[3]—there are simply too many unique queries to tackle much more.

---

[3] Spreadsheet applications typically have a random number generator that will be indispensable here. In Excel, the function is "RAND."

Here are 20 queries in Table 3.2 grabbed from our Michigan State University long tail. In this case, I defined the long tail as queries executed only once; more would have been unwieldy to display in print.

TABLE 3.2

A SAMPLE OF QUERIES FROM MSU'S LONG TAIL				
	Query	Category		Query	Category
1	2007 basketball schedule	date + query	11	main library hours of operation	location + query
2	210e natural resources	location	12	mcgaha	name
3	co op	typo	13	Packaging engineer	
4	co-curricular transcripts		14	powerlifting	
5	courses at msu		15	studend dirctory	typo
6	departemnt of chemistry	typo	16	tuiton	typo
7	farmington hills campus	location	17	urban affairs graduate program lang	program + name
8	freshman year gpa		18	when are grades due	
9	frick	name	19	williams leslie	name
10	jacques	name	20	wilson, sheena	name

The analysis of even such a small sample is informative.

- About 30% of the queries appear to be names of people. This could have huge implications for the MSU search experience, as the university currently uses a separate interface to query the people directory. Perhaps this data makes an argument to combine the two search interfaces into one? Or perhaps teach the search engine to recognize which queries are names and automatically search the directory for entries?

- Fifteen percent of these queries involve locations on campus (or, in the case of Farmington Hills, off campus). Perhaps MSU should consider how easy it is to get directions and maps to its various locations?

- Twenty-five percent of the queries appear to be typos; thank goodness MSU has spellchecking in place!

- Some queries seem really to be combinations of a query and an attribute, like date (for example, 2007 basketball schedule). Considering there are many combinations of queries and attributes (other examples are location, name, and unique identifiers like ISBNs), MSU might consider adding sorting to its search results or exploring moving to a faceted search engine.

- Finally, there are queries that, other than piquing our general curiousity (such as powerlifting?), likely don't merit much more thinking.

Again, *if* you have the time and resources, and have maximized the possibilities of short head analysis, then analyzing long tail queries is worth the effort. The types of queries are simply different than short head—as evidenced by the query/attribute combinations we've noticed, as well as their overall length. (Our 20 long tail terms average 2.45 terms, versus 1.42 for the 50 short head terms we analyzed earlier in this chapter.) You'll be able to use the same pattern analysis techniques, but you'll come away with some different insights.

Anti-Pattern Analysis: Surprises and Outliers

While most of the patterns you find will be at least somewhat predictable, others will be downright head-scratchingly bizarre. For example, years ago some colleagues and I were surprised by a pattern we encountered when analyzing a software company's queries. Many people were searching for URLs. Even more strange, the URLs were for completely different sites. Why on earth would so many people search for a URL, rather than just enter it in their browser's address field?

There were many possible theories, the primary of which was that browsers were still rather new, and users easily confused the two main text entry fields they encountered—the browser's address field and the site's search box. But really, the reason didn't matter that much, because the fix was straightforward: rather than punishing searchers with a "o search results" page, we simply configured the search engine to redirect them to the site they wanted to visit. So, we took a surprising pattern and—rather than toil at making the inscrutable, well, scrutable—we just fixed the problem and improved the users' experience.

You may also encounter queries that just seem to be complete outliers that don't seem to fit within any sort of pattern whatsoever. For example, a quick glance at the short head of many academic sites, like Michigan State University's, will often reveal an odd course ID number (such as CS101) among the queries for football tickets, summer jobs, library hours, and so on.

When you do find a short head query that seems to be an outlier, study it intensely. It may not be an outlier, but simply the harbinger of yet another pattern. Or it may be truly something odd and worthy of investigation. You can find out by digging deeper into the middle torso or do a random sample from the long tail to see if there are many more similar queries showing up.

A Taxonomy of Search Log Junk

Avi Rappoport, Search Tools Consulting—http://searchtools.com/

Search logs contain a lot of weird query lines, and some of them can have a significant effect on how you analyze queries. For example, there's not much sense in knowing that an empty search is your most frequent query, or that computers in China are sending a great many queries, when those are hack attacks on the site. Having looked at hundreds of thousands of lines of search log entries, here are the most frequent and useless, which I call "Search Log Junk" (inspired by Edward Tufte's "chart junk"). Removing these means that site search analytics work on the signal instead of wasting time on the noise.

Empty queries: Searches without words show up all the time in search logs. It's not clear where this comes from: do people click the Search button without typing anything? Does the cursor get into the search field and people click on the Return button? It's still a mystery, but it is very frequent. In any case, including empty queries in search metrics can skew response time (because there's no actual search done) and the numbers for no-matches queries (because an empty search usually retrieves no results).

In this example, there's an IP address, a date and time, and an HTTP GET search request. Usually after the query parameter (q in this case), there should be the words to be searched. Here, there's nothing: an empty search.

```
xxx.xsx.98.144 - - [18/Oct/2010:00:03:25 -0400] "GET /search?q=&la=fi HTTP/1.1" 200 720
    - - 0
```

Repeat queries: Multiple identical queries to the search engine from the same IP or user ID are amazingly frequent. They may be words (sex), random characters (..), or seemingly random queries from mysterious places (author:akr+date:2000/01/01). If the query parameters are slightly different, it usually means that the user is navigating to the next page to check results. But if the query and parameters are identical, and it repeats more than 10 times in 10 minutes, it's likely to be garbage.

```
xxx.xxx.193.166 - - [18/Oct/2010:00:09:44 -0400] "GET /search?q=woman HTTP/1.1" 200
    16205 - "Mozilla/5.0 Galeon/1.2.0 (X11; Linux i686; U;) Gecko/20020326" 426
xxx.xxx.193.166 - - [18/Oct/2010:00:09:58 -0400] "GET /search?q=woman HTTP/1.1" 200
    16205 - "Mozilla/5.0 Galeon/1.2.0 (X11; Linux i686; U;) Gecko/20020326" 426
xxx.xxx.193.166 - - [18/Oct/2010:00:10:26 -0400] "GET /search?q=woman HTTP/1.1" 200
    16205 - "Mozilla/5.0 Galeon/1.2.0 (X11; Linux i686; U;) Gecko/20020326" 426
```

continues on next page

A Taxonomy of Search Log Junk (continued)

Robot crawlers: For public sites, having search and intelligent agents spider the search results is generally good. The search results on your site for emerald green widgets may rank well in Google and Bing results and drive good traffic. Even inside the enterprise, this kind of link can be useful. But if the search robots send constant requests to the search engine, it can skew the statistics, such as the top queries. Robot crawlers identify themselves by using a "User Agent" string, most often with the word "bot" in it. This example shows a request by the Googlebot user agent. So a site search analytics program can include these entries for raw traffic metrics, but exclude them from query and trend reports.

```
xxx.xxx.71.168 - - [18/Oct/2010:11:14:24 -0400] "GET /search?q=emerald-green-
    widgets HTTP/1.1" 200 180 "-" "Mozilla/5.0 (compatible; Googlebot/2.1; +http://www.
    google.com/bot.html)" 199
```

URLs often appear as query terms, mostly to popular sites such as *google.com*, *yahoo. com*, or *facebook.com*, or as in the example below, *myspace.com*. If the site is about these topics, that's fine, but for most sites and especially online stores, they're just noise.

```
xxx.xxx.64.171 - - [11/Oct/2010:11:29:14 -0700] "GET /search?q=myspace.com HTTP/1.0"
    200 1024 "http://example.com/index.html" "Mozilla/4.0 (compatible; MSIE 6.0;MSIE
    7.0; MSIE 8.0; Windows 5.1)" 44
```

Server hacks: Search engines can be attacked by common hacking approaches, such as searches for phpmyadmin and inurl, or calls to the search engine with PUT instead of the customary search request, GET. Very long queries may be attempting buffer overflow and other attacks. And they may succeed, so it's important to work with your security team or webhosting provider to test your search interface against these kinds of attacks.

```
xxx.xxx.0.195 - - [18/Oct/2010:11:22:54 -0400] "GET /search?q=inurl%3Astart.cgi&la=en
    HTTP/1.1" 200 1024 - "Mozilla/2.0" 0
```

Search field spam: There are automated advertising services that insert fake comments with URLs into form fields, guestbooks, blogs, and wikis to get link-backs for better results ranking. This explains why logs contain random queries with sentences, HTML formatting, and URLs in them. They are complete noise and inappropriately raise the number of no-matches searches. It's fairly easy to identify these queries with simple regular expressions looking for href and http, then remove them from the log before processing.

A Taxonomy of Search Log Junk (continued)

```
xxx.xxx.66.180 - - [18/Oct/2010:11:22:54 -0400] "GET /search?q=Beautiful+<a+href=ht
   tp://hotel=ital-oc-example.com>+hotel+italy+ocean+rome</a>&la=it HTTP/1.1" 200 2048
   - "http://www.example.fr" "Mozilla/4.0 (compatible; MSIE 6.0;MSIE 7.0; MSIE 8.0;
   Windows 5.1)" 0
```

Internal testing queries: Automated testing or even heavy manual testing can change the search log significantly, especially given how quickly the long tail shows up. You can remove query entries from certain user IDs or IP addresses if these are stable. My trick for informal testing is to query my own name first and use a specific string such as "Avi's searchtest," which creates an immediate label for my session.

```
xxx.xxx.165.119 - - [18/Oct/2010:11:29:42 -0400] "GET /search?q=searchtest 200 9216 0

xxx.xxx.165.125 - - [18/Oct/2010:11:29:42 -0400] "GET /search?q=testing+123&la=en 200
   16241 224

xxx.xxx.165.125 - - [18/Oct/2010:11:29:49 -0400] "GET /search?q=size+chart&la=en 200
   16002 643330

xxx.xxx.165.119 - - [18/Oct/2010:11:32:47 -0400] "GET /search?q=22 200 9216 0

xxx.xxx.165.127 - - [18/Oct/2010:11:44:00 -0400] "GET /search?q=shipping&la=en
   200 16002 643330
```

Note that in the above example, all the words in "size chart" and "shipping" were in all 643,330 pages on the site.

METRICS

As with everything server-related, it's good to count all the user interactions. The rest of the book is about analyzing search log entries, but tracking the junk entries is important, too. If the search is suddenly painfully slow, it may be an automated system hammering the search engine with repeated queries. If the search engine has problems or crashes, it's good to have the raw numbers of searches, how many had zero matches, recent IP addresses, and trends on the numbers of hits per search. This is particularly important for low-bandwidth situations and hosted site-search services, where each bad interaction may drive up the cost of search.

NICE CLEAN LOGS

Investing in the step of removing the search log junk makes all the analysis in the rest of the book more meaningful. Even for sites with thousands of queries per hour, junk entries can distort statistics such as the percent of searches getting zero matches. Removing the "garbage in" by cleaning this log file data, you can be confident that you're not getting "garbage out."

Summary

- In pattern analysis, you "play" with your data so that common usage patterns, trends, and outliers can emerge.

- To get started, you'll need queries and their corresponding frequency counts. A spreadsheet is often your best tool for analyzing the data.

- You can learn about many different aspects of your searchers' behaviors by analyzing your queries for patterns: nuances in tone, use of synonymous queries, the differences between single and multi-term queries, the impact of time and seasonality, the nature of searchers' information needs, and the kinds of content that they seek.

- You can also perform pattern analysis on a sample of queries that come from the long tail.

- Eliminate search log "junk"—meaningless queries—as best you can to improve your analysis.

CHAPTER 4

Failure Analysis

Study Failure with Care   62
Queries That Return Zero Results   63
Queries That Fail to Retrieve Useful Results   68
Queries That Lead to Immediate Exits from the Site   72
Beyond Generic—Evaluating Failures
   That Mean the Most   74
Summary   77

W hen you're conducting site search analytics, it's incredibly instructive to see where your site's searches are going wrong. While you might be frightened to see how much and how often things go poorly for your site's searchers, SSA can help you quickly figure out where things go wrong so you'll know what to fix first.

Compared to many other types of analysis, you'll find that *failure analysis* is quite simple. You won't have to roll up your sleeves and muck about the guts of your query data quite so much. Instead, you'll generally be able to rely on your web analytics application's "out-of-the-box" reports, many of which already cover some aspect of failure—like that old standby, the "zero search results" report.

Study Failure with Care

But there are two caveats.

First, as we've mentioned before, site search analytics, like other forms of web analytics, can only tell you about behaviors—they can't tell you too much about a user's intent, his reactions, or his feelings. We can't know for certain that, for example, when a searcher retrieves zero results that he definitely failed. It's probably a reasonable bet in most cases, and so we can probably safely define such an outcome as a failure. But there are important exceptions: for example, let's say you're searching a patent information site. In your case, when a query yields zero results, you'd breathe a big sigh of relief. This wasn't a failure, just a happy confirmation that something hadn't already been invented, but a generic zero search results failure report wouldn't explain that. So it's important to define "failure" carefully because your site's context matters. We're making lots of assumptions here simply to demonstrate what is possible with site search analytics.

Second, generic reports describe generic failures. These reports are certainly useful, but treat them as starting points to help you define and analyze failures *on your own terms,* with careful thought about what it means for *your* searchers to fail when trying to do the things that *your site exists to do.* We'll cover a great example of a customized type of failure analysis that Netflix uses at the end of this chapter. But first, let's cover some generic types of failure with a critical eye, many of which you'll find included with common analytics applications.

Queries That Return Zero Results

The most common type of search-related failure is when queries retrieve zero results. Zero search results reports (also called *null results reports*) show the short head of queries—the most common ones—that retrieve nothing. In the following example from Google Analytics,[1] five queries led to null results in the last report period, as shown in Figure 4.1.

Site Search Category	None	Total Un	Total Unique Searches
1. (not set)		6	54.55%
2. no_results		5	45.45%

FIGURE 4.1
There were five no_results queries, according to this Google Analytics report.

Clicking through reveals the five keyword queries that failed to retrieve results in Figure 4.2.

Search Term	None	Total Uni	Total Unique Searches
1. no-results: pasta		1	20.00%
2. no-results: tofu		1	20.00%
3. no-results:apples		1	20.00%
4. no-results:beans		1	20.00%
5. no-results:oranges		1	20.00%

FIGURE 4.2
Sorry, no pasta tofu, apples, beans, or oranges available here!

---

[1] Google Analytics doesn't provide null results reports by default; you'll first need to teach it to recognize your particular site's null result pages. Justin Cutroni explains exactly how to do so here (and this is where we borrowed Figures 6.1 and 6.2 from): http://cutroni.com/blog/2009/09/08/tracking-ero-result-searches-in-google-analytics/

Reducing Thrashing in Zero Search Results Pages

Greg Nudelman, Principal, DesignCaffeine, Inc.—www.DesignCaffeine.com

Author, Design Patterns for Ecommerce Search: Design Secrets and Successful Strategies for Happy Customers (John Wiley, 2011).

Thrashing is a behavioral anti-pattern that occurs when people keep changing their query without removing the problem condition that caused the zero search results to be returned in the first place. Thrashing really frustrates people, and often it results in your potential customers leaving the site without finding what they wanted, creating a very strong negative experience. Analysis of sessions that included zero search results will help you understand and quantify thrashing and design effective strategies to reduce its effects on your site.

To identify cases of thrashing, examine your search data to see what your customers do after they receive zero search results. Pay special attention to sessions where zero search results pages occurred multiple times in a row and then resulted in a customer exiting the site. Some page designs, such as that of Morningstar.com shown in Figure 4.3, unintentionally invite thrashing:

- There is no explicit message that states "No results found." Instead, the tiny font in the black bar states 1-0 of 0, which does not make much sense. Customers that do not know that they have received zero results will likely try the same query several times, which will show up in your analysis.

- Instead of focusing on providing a way out, the page presents several completely useless and confusing links: Analyst Reports & Data, Morningstar Articles, and Tools. At first glance, it seems like clicking these links would let customers browse content relevant to their query. Unfortunately, the links are actually filtering controls that serve only to further constrain a search that already has no results. This leads to thrashing, now requiring the customers to click the Back button. Look for this unnecessary filtering in your analysis.

Reducing Thrashing in Zero Search Results Pages (continued)

- There is very little content on the page that helps customers reach their goal. Most of the links are third-party ads, which have little to do with financial information about Small and Mid Cap Value Funds. Because there is nothing on the page to help them, customers are forced to re-word their query instead. Look for manual query edits in the analysis. This is a prime opportunity to create a better design.

FIGURE 4.3
Morningstar.com
zero results page
design invites
thrashing.

continues on next page

Reducing Thrashing in Zero Search Results Pages (continued)

What can you do once your analysis revealed issues or opportunities for improvement?

- Use spelling correction and substitute a searcher's original keywords with different keywords from a controlled vocabulary.

- Remove some of a customer's original keywords from the query or make partial matches.

- Match only categories or facets, without the keywords.

- Display top searches, featured results, or most popular results.

I usually counsel minimizing third-party resources and ads on zero search results pages. However, if your site does not carry the product your customers are looking for, third-party ads may be an effective strategy of last resort and provide a positive experience to your customers.

Successful strategies for handling cases when there are no search results are not limited to the four I've just mentioned. For example, Google's brilliant auto-suggest feature is an excellent example of a successful marriage of two strategies: making partial keyword matches and using a controlled vocabulary for keyword substitution. By matching the beginning of a string, the customer begins to type with popular search keywords. Google fosters a successful search, forestalling the no-search-results condition before it ever occurs.

On the zero search results pages, don't stick with just one specific type of search assistance. Instead, get creative—combine design features and content in a way that best meets the goals of your partner in conversation on the other side of the human-computer interface.

You're Not Offering What People Want

Does this data suggest that you offer more products or services? If searchers are already coming to your site with the perception, however unfounded, that you may already offer the item they're searching for, *maybe you should*. Of course, just because someone searches for a Uranium P32 Space Modulator doesn't necessarily mean you should offer it, especially if your business and site offers hypnotherapy services.

The key is to focus on queries that are potentially relevant to your business and monitor them for both volume and a rate of growth that might make them worthwhile to bring to the attention of your colleagues in marketing and R&D. Your data-driven trend spotting might be doing them a huge favor (and saving them a lot of money in comparison to conventional product and market analysis).

The Content's There but Isn't Being Found

This happens more often than you'd think or like. Fortunately, the problem is that your "missing content" is most likely just not being indexed properly by your search engine. This is an easy fix: point the search engine in the right direction to find the content and that should take care of the issue.

The "missing content" problem happens most often in two cases: (1) stores of non-HTML documents (PDFs, MS Word documents, and so on) that your search engine simply might not know to index; and, surprisingly (2) ecommerce sites, where search engines are geared toward indexing product data rather than HTML content. In both cases, there are fairly straightforward technical fixes that can be accomplished through reconfiguring your search engine.

There's a Disconnect Between Your Site's Content and the People Using It

The language your searchers use doesn't match the language in your content, and sadly, your search engine can't play matchmaker. This is a warning sign to slow down, regroup, and align your content. Spend some time reconsidering your titling guidelines you ask your content authors and editors to follow. Rethink the metadata you ask them to use to describe the content. Show them the kinds of terms searchers use, how those terms differ from the language used in the prose, and how that disconnect leads to their content not getting found.

Now that you know which queries aren't retrieving results, you're ready for the analysis that will lead, hopefully, to some useful hypotheses. Here are a few likely explanations to follow up.

Queries That Fail to Retrieve Useful Results

When can you tell that a search has failed? (Aside, of course, from the case we've just described, where no results were retrieved.)

The answer, of course, depends on a variety of factors that are difficult to predict. The search algorithm may not do a good job of parsing the searcher's query. The query may have retrieved good results, but the results aren't presented in a usable way. The results might be usable, but your site's searchers are an impatient gang who are unwilling to scroll or click through long lists of search results.

The first two examples are, respectively, examples of challenges that are technical and design-related. They're areas that are within your control, and as such, you can address and correct them.

But the searchers? Not so much. And in most cases, your site's searchers are as impatient, unforgiving, and lazy as they come. They'll expect instant gratification at the top of the first page of search results. That's why we suggest making it your goal to ensure that the first page of results contains as many relevant results as your content will bear. Anything less should be considered a failure.

Are the Top Results Relevant?

You can try the same precision-based approach as The Vanguard Group used in Chapter 1, "How Site Search Analysis Can Save Your Butt." To refresh your memory, John Ferrara and his colleagues analyzed just the *top five results* for their common queries. They assumed that most searchers' level of attention would degrade after the first five results.

Then they rated each result's relevance using one of these four ratings:

- **Relevant (r):** Based on the information the searcher provided, the result's ranking is completely relevant.

- **Near (n):** The result is not a perfect match, but it's clearly reasonable for it to be ranked highly.

- **Misplaced (m):** It's reasonable for the search engine to have retrieved the result, but it shouldn't be ranked highly.

- **Irrelevant (i):** The result has no apparent relationship to the query.

John and his colleagues tallied their evaluations in the spreadsheet shown in Figure 4.4. Each row is a common query, and the columns correspond to the top five results for each query.

	A	B	C	D	E	F
1	Query string	Result 1	Result 2	Result 3	Result 4	Result 5
2	reserve room	r	n	n	r	m
3	software install	n	m	n	i	i
4	personal plan	m	n	i	i	n
5	pto	r	n	n	m	n
6	united way	m	m	m	m	m
7	visitor	m	i	n	r	n
8	morgan galley	r	r	m	n	n
9	referral	m	n	m	i	i
10	large transaction	m	i	i	i	i
11	closed funds	m	m	i	n	i
12	key request	r	m	n	m	i
13	irvs	m	m	m	n	m
14	holidays	r	m	m	i	n
15	ship shape	r	n	n	r	n
16	training	m	i	m	i	n

FIGURE 4.4

Each common query's top five results were rated as "r" (for relevant), "n" (for nearly relevant), "m" (for misplaced), and "i" (for irrelevant).

John then used the relevance ratings as the basis of scoring the search results. He did this in three separate ways: strict, loose, and permissive:

- **Strict:** Only results ranked as *relevant* were acceptable (r).

- **Loose:** Both *relevant* and *near* results were counted (r+n).

- **Permissive:** *Relevant, near,* and *misplaced* results were counted (r+n+m).

So, the query "reserve room," by *strict* definition, scored a 40%—two of the five results were rated an "r." By *loose* definition, it scored an 80%. (Four of the five results were rated "r" or "n.") And by *permissive* definition, it scored a 100%. (None of the results were rated an "i.") You can see how all the results fared in Figure 4.5.

FIGURE 4.5
The precision of each
query's results was
then scored in three
different ways (strict,
loose, and permissive).

	A	B	C	D	E	F	G	H	I
1	Query string	Result 1	Result 2	Result 3	Result 4	Result 5	Precision (strict)	Precision (loose)	Precision (permissive)
2	reserve room	r	n	n	r	m	40%	80%	100%
3	software install	n	m	n	i	i	0%	40%	60%
4	personal plan	m	n	i	i	n	0%	40%	60%
5	pto	r	n	n	m	n	20%	80%	100%
6	united way	m	m	m	m	m	0%	0%	100%
7	visitor	m	i	n	r	n	20%	60%	80%
8	morgan galley	r	r	m	n	n	40%	80%	100%
9	referral	m	n	m	n	i	0%	20%	60%
10	large transaction	m	i	i	i	i	0%	0%	20%
11	closed funds	m	m	i	n	i	0%	20%	60%
12	key request	r	m	n	m	r	20%	40%	80%
13	irs	m	m	m	n	m	0%	20%	100%
14	holidays	r	m	m	i	n	20%	40%	80%
15	ship shape	r	n	n	r	n	40%	100%	100%
16	training	m	i	m	i	n	0%	20%	60%

In the Vanguard example, three different metrics were used to evaluate the top five search results for common queries. We can quickly see that certain individual queries are failing—no matter which of the three metrics we use—like large transaction. That's why using multiple metrics as part of a single analysis is helpful; you know a query has failed when it fails not one, not two, but all three of these tests.

You can now consider applying this same approach to failure analysis *collectively* to your queries. For example, you might decide to make sure that the top 15 most frequent queries collectively receive a passing grade. You then set thresholds for failure, deciding that those 15 queries should collectively average 55% on strict terms, 75% on loose terms, and 95% on permissive terms. Now that your thresholds are in place, you can track performance over time, as Vanguard did, and eventually bring performance above "failure" levels.

Is the "Best Match" Near the Top of the Search Results?

Here's another way to make sure your top results aren't failing. You'll remember, from Chapter 1, that Vanguard also measured for top queries' relevancy by making sure the "best" match for a query was retrieved at or close to the top of the first search results page. These relevancy metrics work only with queries that actually have a "best match" result—and by no means does every query have one. But when they do, you can determine how often a best match shows up in, say, the top five search results for a particular query. And if it doesn't? Consider it a failure.

When Vanguard tested those among its common queries known to have "best matches," it found a lot of successes and some notable failures. For example, the best match for the query job descriptions was in the lowly position of #79; ideally, it should have been at #1 (see Figure 4.6).

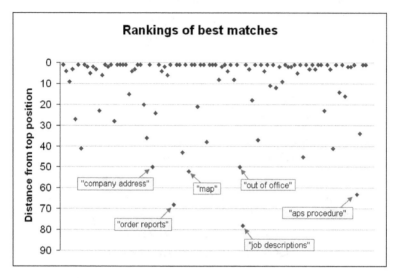

FIGURE 4.6
"Best matches" for Vanguard's frequent queries—many don't occur in the top five search results positions.

As with the precision metrics, none is ideal on its own, but collectively they paint a more complete picture of performance. And as with precision, you can use these metrics to evaluate the collective performance of your short head queries.

Are Results Being Clicked at a Healthy Rate?

If you have clickstream data, you can use it in combination with your site search data to measure a very similar metric: *selection rate*. Selection rate is simply defined as the percentage of clicks that a piece of content gets for a specific query.

For example, let's say that result #23 of a query's 675 results happens to be the most clicked result with a whopping selection rate of 19%. That means searchers are digging pretty deep into this query's search results to find something that (we think) they must really like—after all, they click through to it quite frequently. In effect, they're telling you that the query's best match is #23. You can now assume it is indeed the "best match"—and look into ways to move it up toward result #1—in just the same way that Vanguard did.

Queries That Lead to Immediate Exits from the Site

Poor search results can drive searchers crazy and, in the process, drive them away from your site. *Search exits* happen when searchers leave after retrieving results for a query without clicking on *any* results. Let's have a look at AIGA's search exits percentages within its short head queries in Google Analytics: note that 19.82% of the queries, on average, were immediately exited. In Figure 4.7, the table's far right column shows the exit rate for each unique query's individual search exit percentage

Total Unique Searches (?)	Results Pageviews/Search (?)	% Search Exits (?)	% Search Refinements (?)
14,500	**1.58**	**19.82%**	**19.41%**
% of Site Total: 100.00%	Site Avg: 1.58 (0.00%)	Site Avg: 19.82% (0.00%)	Site Avg: 19.41% (0.00%)

	Search Term ⌄	None ⌄	Total Unique ↓ Searches	Results Pageviews/Search	% Search Exits
1.	case study		203	1.37	57.64%
2.	salary		140	1.33	5.00%
3.	resume		103	2.10	11.65%
4.	portfolio		85	1.86	9.41%
5.	internships		83	1.35	10.84%

FIGURE 4.7
Most frequent AIGA.
org queries and their
percentages of search
exits.

You'll notice that the biggest offender was also the most common query during this period: case study had a much higher search exit percentage (57.64%) than average. The second most common query, salary, had a low search exit percentage of 5%. Let's compare the results for each; here are the top search results for case study, as shown in Figure 4.8.

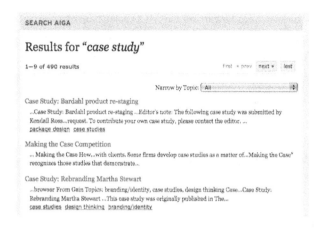

SEARCH AIGA

Results for "*case study*"

1—9 of 490 results   first · prev next · last

Narrow by Topic: [All   ]

Case Study: Bardahl product re-staging
    ...Case Study: Bardahl product re-staging ...Editor's note: The following case study was submitted by
    Kendall Ross...request. To contribute your own case study, please contact the editor. ...
    package design case studies

Making the Case Competition
    ... Making the Case How...with clients. Some firms develop case studies as a matter of...Making the Case"
    recognizes those studies that demonstrate...

Case Study: Rebranding Martha Stewart
    ...browser From Gain Topics: branding/identity, case studies, design thinking Case...Case Study:
    Rebranding Martha Stewart ...This case study was originally published in The...
    case studies design thinking branding/identity

FIGURE 4.8
Search results for case
study at AIGA.org.

Notice that these results cover a wide range of case studies. Some, like Making the Case Competition, aren't so much about case studies as about making the case for design in general. Perhaps the wide variety of results throws off searchers, who may have been expecting a broader treatment of case study-related content. (Along those lines, AIGA might be able to fix the problem simply by creating some sort of overview page for its case studies and making sure it came up in position #1 for the queries case study and case studies.)

By contrast, here are the results for the search salary in Figure 4.9.

SEARCH AIGA

Results for "*salary*"

1—9 of 139 results   first · prev next · last

Narrow by Topic: [All   ]

Annual salary survey reveals opportunities for the design industry amid modest wage ...
    ...press releases Annual salary survey reveals opportunities for the design industry amid...modest wage
    increases AIGA and Aquent release comprehensive salary survey data for the U.S. communication
    design...
    career salaries jobs professional issues

AIGA|Aquent Salary Survey
    ...Resources AIGA|Aquent Salary Survey The...with Communication Arts magazine. The salary survey is
    part of a...well as to use the interactive Salary Calculator. As a benefit of membership...
    salaries

AIGA Design Educators Salary Survey
    ... AIGA Design Educators Salary Survey AIGA...AIGA Design Educators Salary Survey 2008 was
    published online...Salary/wages overview ...
    salaries educators

FIGURE 4.9
Search results for
salary at AIGA.org.

These results deal almost entirely with annual AIGA salary surveys, and perhaps search exits are lower here because searchers are generally more interested in finding a single year's survey and can safely and easily ignore the rest.

As you can see from these examples, it's most useful to analyze percentages of search exits for common queries that range far from the overall averages. Glance through them on a regular basis, and you'll find it hard not to notice the queries with high percentages of search exits—the queries that really failed your site's searchers.

Beyond Generic— Evaluating Failures That Mean the Most

The types of failures we've examined in this chapter are fairly generic and, as noted, are often handled by existing reports in common analytics applications. "Generic failures" are useful, but you might see them as springboards toward more specialized failure analyses that make sense, given your organization's unique business goals. In other words, investigate "meaningful failure" as much as you can.

The following example of how to measure and evaluate meaningful failure comes from Netflix, the movie and TV show subscription service (see Figure 4.10). We should note that it includes both query data *and* clickstream data, integrating them quite gracefully. Here's what the chart below includes:

- **Query Count:** The number of times a query was entered within a specific period of time. Almost always, a query is the title of a movie or TV show.

- **MDP Views:** The number of times a search result was clicked through.

- **MDP Views per Query:** The rate at which each query's results were clicked through.

- **Queue Adds:** The number of times a clicked-through result was added to the subscribers' queues of shows to rent.

- **Queue Adds per Query:** The percentage at which a clicked-through show was added to the queue.

- **Query:** The term that was actually searched.

Query Count	MDP Views	MDP Views per Query	Queue Adds	Queue Adds per Query	Query
20762	2394	11.53% |||	1625	7.83% ||||||	click
9360	1521	16.25% ||||	780	8.33% |||||||	the departed
8756	2114	24.14% |||||	909	10.38% |||||||||	thank you for smoking
7545	1555	20.61% |||||	563	7.46% |||||||	over the hedge
3746	1140	30.43% |||||||	261	6.97% ||||||	cars
3318	569	17.15% |||	259	7.81% |||||||	departed
3246	1004	30.93% |||||||	305	9.40% ||||||||	x-men
3157	928	29.40% |||||	258	8.17% ||||||||	xmen
3107	776	24.98% ||||	268	8.63% ||||||||	x men
3002	1671	55.66% |||||||||||	121	4.03% ||||	lost
2970	505	17.00% |||	220	7.41% |||||||	the lake house
2811	388	13.80% ||	206	7.33% |||||||	employee of the month
2766	287	10.38% ||	209	7.56% |||||||	open season
2675	246	9.20% |	186	6.95% ||||||	the guardian
2599	413	15.89% |||	154	5.93% |||||	waist deep
2598	343	13.20% ||	284	10.93% |||||||||	the queen
2461	556	22.59% ||||	220	8.94% ||||||||	little miss sunshine
2328	512	21.99% ||||	171	7.35% |||||||	lake house

FIGURE 4.10

Netflix data showing frequent queries, their click-through rates, and their rates of being added to subscribers' queues.

To dig deeper into the analysis, consider *Query Count* as a popularity measure. For example, *Thank You for Smoking* is the third most popular movie, having been searched for 8,756 times during this time period.

Ditto *MDP Views per Query:* subscribers click through at high rates to learn more. In the case of *Thank You for Smoking*, they clicked through at a relatively high rate: 24.14%.

And the same is true of *Queue Adds per Query:* the movie was added to subscribers' queues at the relatively high rate of 10.38%.

To boil this down, *Thank You for Smoking* is a great success from Netflix's perspective: it was searched for at a high rate, clicked through at a high rate, and added to queues at a high rate.

But Netflix is much more concerned about failures. For example, *Lost* was the 10th most frequently searched query (a robust 3,002 times). It was frequently clicked through (at an impressive 55.66% rate), but only added to queues 4.03% of the time. It's pretty safe to say that this query is a failure, and it would be important for Netflix to follow up on it and learn what was going wrong. (Hypotheses? TV shows have multiple results, as opposed to movies, that might require a lot of scrolling and simply be confusing to searchers who are looking for a specific episode. Or the word "lost" comes up in a lot of other titles of shows and movies. Whatever the case, Netflix would now have some good ideas about what needed to be fixed.)

This is a great method for looking for important failures if you're in the movie subscription business, like Netflix. It's highly unlikely that it would work for your organization. But given the business you're in: what kinds of failures are important for *you* to investigate? If you can work that through, your query data—when combined with other types of data—will help you do just that.

Summary

- Failure analysis helps you diagnose problems and determine what to fix or improve for your site's searchers.

- Queries that lead to zero results usually suggest that

  - You aren't offering the content that your searchers want.

  - You offer it, but the search engine isn't finding it.

  - A difference exists between how you and your searchers describe the same content.

- Queries that fail to retrieve useful results or lead to immediate exits from your site are other decent indicators of failure.

- Go beyond out-of-the-box reports and their generic definitions of failure, and try to determine custom definitions that correspond to the needs of your own site's users—and for your organization.

CHAPTER 5

Session Analysis

Learning from Who Searched What and When   80

Why Analyze Sessions?   83

What's a Session, Anyway?   83

Analyzing a Short Session from TFANet   84

Analyzing a Long Session from WW Norton   86

Which Sessions Should You Analyze?   89

How Granular Are Your Terms?   90

Going Beyond Sessions:

    Looking at Individual Searchers   92

Summary   94

I n site search analytics, we generally analyze individual search queries. But how about exploring what happens during search *sessions*—where a searcher executes multiple queries as he tries to address a single information need?

Most search engines and analytics applications don't tell you much about *who*—which specific individual, rather than which audience—is the source of a query. There may be technical reasons for this, or a laudable desire to protect users' privacy. But, occasionally, you will, in fact, know *who* searches *what*—most typically, on your intranet or in some other similarly closed environment. When you have this opportunity, make the most of it by studying searchers' sessions: what goes on starting from an initial query and finishing with a completed search experience. Besides being one more analytical tool in your toolkit, it will tell you more about searchers' information needs; specifically, how those needs evolve as the searcher interacts with search results and actual content.

Learning from Who Searched What and When

The following snippet of session data comes from TFANet, an extranet managed by Teach For America, an education non-profit that recruits college graduates to serve two-year assignments teaching in the country's poorest urban and rural schools. TFANet provides resources to improve teaching performance and provide career guidance to its members during and after their life in the TFA Corps.

In Figure 5.1, "Person ID" shows *who* searched, "SEARCH FOR" column shows *what* they searched for, and "DATE," which is how the data is sorted, shows *when*.

"TFAPERSONTYPE"—the *kind* of TFA person doing the searching[1]—and "TFACURRENTCMREGIONNAME"—*where* they are located—will be of greatest interest to the analysts who actually work at TFA—and to those doing audience analysis (which I'll cover in Chapter 7, "Goal-Based Analysis").

---

[1] "CM" means Corps Members—TFA teachers. "ALUM" means alumni of the TFA Corps. All other types are TFA staff.

Time Period: 5/17/2010 - 6/17/2010				
Person ID	TFAPERSONTYPE	TFACURRENTCMREGIONNAME	SEARCH FOR	DATE
2632365	CM	Houston	texes testing	5/17/10 0:25
2632365	CM	Houston	texes testing	5/17/10 0:25
2497096	APPLICANT	Los Angeles	los angeles	5/17/10 2:56
2564148	CM	Colorado	colorado	5/17/10 4:44
2031391	CM	Baltimore	school counseling	5/17/10 8:37
2557633	CM	Dallas	texes testing	5/17/10 10:13
2557633	CM	Dallas	texes testing	5/17/10 10:13
2323237	CM	Miami-Dade	miami	5/17/10 10:19
2472030	APPLICANT	Indianapolis	2010	5/17/10 10:30
2445146	CM	Mississippi Delta	delta	5/17/10 11:11
1087171	ALUM	Eastern North Carolina	survey alumni	5/17/10 11:32
2473030	CM	South Dakota	South Dakota	5/17/10 11:50
2091304	ASSOCIATE	(null)	2010 newark corps community	5/17/10 12:29
2574767	APPLICANT	Bay Area	resume	5/17/10 13:40
1934941	CM	South Louisiana	alumni	5/17/10 14:16
2068291	ASSOCIATE	New York City	louis	5/17/10 14:21
2068291	ASSOCIATE	New York City	louis	5/17/10 14:21
1507413	ALUM	Charlotte	charlotte	5/17/10 14:29
2174172	CM	Houston	texes testing	5/17/10 14:56
2174172	CM	Houston	texes testing	5/17/10 14:57
1091153	ALUM	Rio Grande Valley	take one	5/17/10 15:53
1091153	ALUM	Rio Grande Valley	NBPTS	5/17/10 15:54
2633864	CM	Dallas	90005	5/17/10 17:37
2483379	CM	Greater New Orleans	pre-institute work	5/17/10 18:14
2483379	CM	Greater New Orleans	pre-institute work	5/17/10 18:15

FIGURE 5.1

This query data sample, from a Teach For America intranet, includes searchers' ID numbers and time/date stamping; together, these enable session parsing.

Here we're focused on using the *who* and *when* information to identify sessions. We can then look at sessions that match individual searchers. (Please also note that the original data set included searchers' names, but I've hidden that to protect their privacy. If you're in a similar position, you should always do the same.)

The Excel pixies pay us a visit, helping us get the data into shape for sussing out sessions. Their work is pretty straightforward: sort first by Person ID and then by TIME. Then it's our turn. After a quick visual scan, we find sessions beginning to emerge. Here's an example in Figure 5.2 of a specific session: one searcher from the Mississippi Delta regions entering queries over a two-minute period on May 21, 2010.

1075914	ALUM	Mississippi Delta	law	5/21/10 10:44
1075914	ALUM	Mississippi Delta	law	5/21/10 10:45
1075914	ALUM	Mississippi Delta	detroit	5/21/10 10:45
1075914	ALUM	Mississippi Delta	sail	5/21/10 10:46

FIGURE 5.2

A session. On May 21, 2010, over the course of a few minutes, searcher #1075914 (a TFA alum from the Mississippi Delta region) searched for law, detroit, and sail. Hmmm...

What exactly was the searcher, a TFA alum, thinking here? In the space of no more than two minutes, that person searched twice for law, then once each for detroit (even though she is based in the Mississippi Delta region), and, um, sail. Strange? Yes, and this is where subject matter expertise is required. I asked Laura Zingg, a business analyst at Teach For America, if she could interpret what was going on during this session—if it was, indeed, a single search session—or two or three squeezed rapid-fire into a tight time window.

Laura also found it perplexing but was fascinated by this close-up view of what was going on inside the TFANet alum's head. Her educated guess: the searcher was probably looking for other alumni who were practicing "law" in "Detroit," maybe in anticipation of a move to the Detroit area.

Laura wondered why the searcher didn't simply put detroit and law together in a single query. Is this a pattern? That's something that further data analysis could answer. Is it unclear that the interface is able to handle multiple-term queries? Or maybe the entry box isn't wide enough? If so, perhaps it could be addressed through educating searchers or incorporating query-building guidance directly into the search interface or making the box wider. Or perhaps searchers don't understand how the search system processes queries at all. Good questions—and possible answers—begin to emerge.

As far as sail goes, Laura confessed that she had to really stretch to even come up with any sort of hypothesis at all. Perhaps the searcher might have hoped to find another alum in Detroit who shared a love for sailing. Or any TFA alum who liked to sail.

Here are some other possibilities: the searcher misspelled a word, like fail, which the engine assumed was sail. (In which case, we'll give it an "F" for "fail.") Or perhaps that person just was curious to see if anything at all came up when she typed in her favorite activity. Whatever it was, her search for the Holy Sail may not have concluded well, but when we analyze the data, it certainly gets us thinking in a constructive way. (As it did for Laura. Thanks, Laura!)

Why Analyze Sessions?

As you can see, session analysis provides yet one more way to learn from your query data, and naturally, it's always useful to have one more option in your toolkit. It can show you how searchers refine their queries, and by extension, how their *information needs* change over a short period of time (a session), rather than what's happening with individual, disconnected queries. As with the other types of analysis I'll cover here, it's easy to jump in—you play with the data and look for interesting patterns and surprises.

Indeed, that's the special sauce of session analysis: you focus on the *searcher's need* rather than the *query*. You can learn how the searcher understands his own need, and how that understanding changes as he interacts with your site's search results and content. By contextualizing individual queries, session analysis affords you a much closer connection to what the searcher experiences when interacting with your search system. For example, you can gain new perspective on why certain queries fail, or why it is that those weird query types keep showing up in your logs. You can get a sense of how important queries—say common ones, or specific ones, like product searches—perform in a broader context. And you can learn how narrow queries get before they succeed in retrieving content—or before the searcher gives up altogether.

Studying information needs is really a better way to understand *how* people really search when compared with analyzing individual queries, if you can pull it off. There are some limitations, of course; chief among them is being able to define what a session actually *is*.

What's a Session, Anyway?

A session is a searcher's time-constrained effort to satisfy an information need. Put differently, it's a search for a single type of information within a specific period of time. Put yet one more way, a session is a weasel. A session is hard to pin down because its definition hinges on two tricky, *weaselly* variables: a *need* and a *time period*.

An information need can and often will change during a session. Let's say you started out searching your employer's intranet for help with understanding your pension plan. You ended up with the name of someone who might be an expert in your company's human resource policies. What happened between those queries might be obvious to you, but how you got from Point A (pension plan) to Point B (Susan Landsman) won't likely be at all obvious to someone analyzing the query data.

In fact, it's very likely the session isn't done. For a variety of reasons—perhaps Susan Landsman isn't the expert you'd hoped for, or she gives you some better terms to search—your journey may have only just begun. So you may continue searching tomorrow. Or next week, after you're back from vacation. Is this morning's search for pension plan and the same query repeated next week the same session?

As is the case in all things weasel, compromises must be made. For purposes of your analysis, you might define a session's time constraints by requiring consecutive queries to be made no more than one hour apart. Or 10 minutes apart. It will really depend on your understanding of the context in which users are interacting with your site. Queries made from a desktop computer might be made in more rapid succession than ones made from a tablet on the factory floor.

And you might also say that a session's queries have to *appear* related. This is much harder to determine. You may not, for example, have any idea that Susan Landsman knows anything about pension policies.

Analyzing a Short Session from TFANet

I scanned the Teach For America data for instances of common queries that occurred in sessions, such as Delta ICEG (an "Investment, Community, and Execution Group," which helps with professional development in particular regions, in this case in the Delta region). It didn't take long to spot a two-query session that repeated itself multiple times. Here, searchers #2123288 and #1963366, both Corps members (CM), followed up their initial queries with a search for delta learning team, as shown in Figures 5.3–5.4.

| 2123288 | CM | Mississippi Delta | Delta ICEG | 5/23/10 11:29 |
| 2123288 | CM | Mississippi Delta | delta learning team | 5/23/10 11:30 |

FIGURE 5.3
Searcher #2123288 first searched Delta ICEG, then
delta learning team...

| 1963366 | CM | Mississippi Delta | delta iceg | 5/30/10 14:27 |
| 1963366 | CM | Mississippi Delta | delta learning team | 5/30/10 14:28 |

FIGURE 5.4
...as did searcher #1963366.

While scanning the data, I noticed a similar case: searcher #2123492—yet
another Corps member—initially searched for ICEG rather than Delta ICEG
(see Figure 5.5).

| 2123492 | CM | Mississippi Delta | ICEG | 5/23/10 9:51 |
| 2123492 | CM | Mississippi Delta | Delta Learning Team | 5/23/10 9:51 |

FIGURE 5.5
Searcher #2123492 exhibited almost exactly the same query
progression as did searchers #2123288 and #1963366.

So what is going on with all these searches for Teach For America's Delta
ICEG? And why do searchers keep following it up with Delta learning team?

When I showed her these sessions, Laura Zingg immediately could tell that
searches for Delta ICEG were retrieving unusually awful results (see Figure 5.6).

FIGURE 5.6
The best result for the
search Delta ICEG is
nowhere to be seen...

In fact, the best result doesn't show up until position #9 (of the 10 results shown) in Figure 5.7.

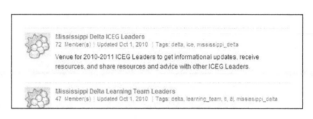

FIGURE 5.7
...until position #9 of
the 10 search results.

Why is that? After Laura investigated further, she found a problem with how weighting had been configured in the search engine's relevance ranking algorithm. TFA communities (like ICEG) rise to the top of the results based on how recently their content has been refreshed. It's apparently been awhile since the Delta ICEG content was updated, so searchers, who were expecting it to be higher, were likely to have been unpleasantly surprised.

So why did they search for Delta learning team next? Laura guesses that searchers considered it an alternative to Delta ICEG. Only problem is that, though they're similar, they're not the same thing. And so searchers still wouldn't find what they were looking for.

The lesson here? Simple: a little data—just a two-query session—can go a long way. Analyzing just a small snippet of session data led to reevaluating how the search engine's weighting was configured. TFANet staff can now start making a case to invest resources into a relatively small task, one that could make a great impact on the site's search experience.

Analyzing a Long Session from WW Norton

Book publisher WW Norton's site supported an interesting implementation of search—users were required to classify their queries as either titles, authors, or ISBNs from the initial query entry interface, as shown in Figure 5.8.

FIGURE 5.8
WW Norton's old book
search UI classified
queries as title
searches by default.
You could change it
to author or ISBN.
Complicated, and that's
not even getting into
the keyword search UI.

I would never bless an interface that would make it so difficult to enter
an initial query. (It should be noted that WW Norton has dramatically
improved its search system since I looked over its data.) However, knowing
query types in advance did make the analysis especially interesting. Not
only could I see *what* people searched, but also the important *attributes* of
what they were searching for and how they changed within a session.

After poring through the data for a couple hours, I showed some of the
more interesting sessions I'd discovered to the Web team at WW Norton
(see Figure 5.9). This one really caught their attention; not surprisingly, it
was the hardest for us non-subject matter experts to figure out.

4/24/07 9:27 AM	title	norton anthology of amer lit	
4/24/07 9:28 AM	isbn	0-393-92742-3	ISBN for the *Norton Anthology of American Literature, 7th ed, vol D*
4/24/07 10:03 AM	title	norton anthology of american literature	
4/24/07 10:09 AM	title	0-393-92743-1	ISBN for the *Norton Anthology of American Literature, 7th ed, vol E*
4/24/07 10:11 AM	isbn	norton anthology of american lit	
4/24/07 10:12 AM	isbn	392739	Why searching partial ISBN? (Is that what it is?)
4/24/07 10:12 AM	isbn	39273	Why searching partial ISBN? (Is that what it is?)
4/24/07 10:12 AM	author	baymina	should be "nina baym" (editor)
4/24/07 10:13 AM	author	baymina	Repeated; why?
4/24/07 10:14 AM	title	norton anthology	

FIGURE 5.9
One user's search session at the WW Norton site. Queries (in red) are
classified in the second column; I listed my questions in the right column.

Together, we pieced what had happened this way:

The searcher started out by searching for norton anthology of amer lit, a shortened version of a popular Norton book's title. He quickly followed that up with an ISBN search and retrieved a specific volume from a specific edition. A little while later, the user searched with the full title. Is it the same session? We can't be certain. Why did the user search again, and why the full title this time?

The user then searched for a specific edition's ISBN—only this time, as a title. This was almost certainly an error, and the Norton search engine was quite unforgiving in such situations, returning poor results and leading the searcher to flail about for the next few minutes. The user next searched the title as an ISBN and then tried some ISBN fragments.

Then the user tried an author search—twice—for baymina, which is likely a misremembered juxtaposition of the editor's name (Nina Baym). Finally, the poor searcher tried a very simple query for norton anthology, which was almost too general to be of value when searching the Norton catalog.

Ooof. Lots happening here, almost too much, and not all of it is by any means good. What did we learn?

- **This search system is likely broken.** Given that searchers tried to find the same book—on a publisher's site, nonetheless—and used multiple attributes (title, ISBN, and author), it's a fair hypothesis that the basic search *ain't* working. Other sessions and testing the queries' performance seemed to bear this out.

- **It's dangerous to require users to classify their own queries.** The default you choose (for example, title) may not be suitable, and either way, people will miss it again and again. In at least two cases in this single session, it seems pretty clear that query classification introduced a major error.[2]

---

2 In fact, I later looked at all title searches and found that roughly one-third were ISBNs or author names.

- **Users repeat exactly the same queries.** Do they really expect something different to come up? Are they insane? Probably not. Many engines treat the loading of each new page of search results as the execution of a query. It's almost certain that your session data will show duplicated results, so you should know why: your search engine is the likely culprit.

- **Search results design can almost always be improved.** Here, the searcher *knew what he was looking for*. Even then, the engine's search results design didn't make it easy to understand that there were different volumes and editions to contend with. It didn't make it clear who the editor was. The searcher had a fuzzy memory of Nina Baym's name but should have found it spelled out exactly within the search results.

If you're thinking that this is quite a bit to infer from a single session, you'd be right. But that's the point: if one session can tell you so much, think of what happens when you start reviewing multiple sessions and detecting broader patterns? In the next section, I'll suggest some ways to select larger numbers of sessions to analyze.

Which Sessions Should You Analyze?

It's almost certain that your data contains more sessions than you'd ever want to analyze or have the time for. You could dive in and grab a random sample of 10 or 20 sessions for an initial exploration. You'll definitely get up close and personal with your query data and, indirectly, your searchers. You'll not only learn a bit about session analysis first-hand, but you'll pick up something of value about your site's sessions specifically.

But it's quite likely that you'd be overwhelmed by the sheer volume of data before any meaningful patterns truly emerged. So instead, I suggest culling a few critical session *types* from your data and focusing on them. Here are a few session types that you might consider to drive your sampling:

- **Sessions that include most frequent queries.** You could be even more specific, looking at sessions that *start* with common queries separately from those that *end* with them.

- **Sessions that include an interesting query type.** These "interesting" queries might be specialized queries like names, product IDs, dates, or other types of searchers that are very important within the context of your site—in other words, the queries that are really important to understand. How do sessions that include those interesting query types go?

- **Sessions that end in failure.** For example, do you see a pattern among sessions that end with no results? Are there signs at the *start* of sessions that are tip-offs for eventual failure?

How Granular Are Your Terms?

As you analyze sessions, look for changes in granularity; that is, how broad or specific the query's meaning is. Do you see a pattern that shows searchers progressively narrowing queries, say from bicycle to tandem bike? Or vice versa? Is there a natural "resting place" where searchers don't get more specific—a point at which they've moved from molecules to atoms?

Knowing the "right" level of granularity can be useful for developing sufficiently narrow metadata and for encouraging those who apply metadata to your organization's content to go equally narrow. One of the biggest barriers to successfully applying metadata is that many content owners use terms that are simply too broad—like tagging their document as being about "higher education" when it's being included in a site dedicated to education. Here's an opportunity to show them that if searchers think in far more specific terms, then so should they.

There's another possible benefit to derive from having a good sense of term granularity, one that might help you save a lot of money in Search Engine Optimization (SEO) efforts. Given that most Web advertising opportunities—like Google AdWords—require you to bid on keywords for position, you'll be bidding with many competitors if you only know how to bid on broader keywords. If you determine narrower keywords, you'll have less competition. Where might you find such narrower keywords? Your site's searchers, of course!

For example, you can see from the following sample of Michigan State University's data in Figure 5.10 that "referral queries"—ones that come from Web search engines like Google—are coarser than those from the local search engine.

Michigan State University, September 2006								
Referral Queries			**Local Queries**					
Query	Count	Percent	Query	Count	Percent			
michigan state	39165	21.33%	football	5891	1.24%			
msu	17940	9.77%	library	5382	1.13%			
michigan state	17357	9.45%	campus+map	3897	0.82%			
msu.edu	5251	2.86%	angel	3891	0.82%			
(other)	3958	2.16%	im+west	3847	0.81%			
campus map	2137	1.16%	map	3794	0.80%		MSU name	
www.msu.edu	1898	1.03%	study+abroad	3490	0.73%		sports	
map	1723	0.94%	football+sched	3122	0.66%		map	
michigan	880	0.48%	spartantrak	2689	0.57%		surprises	
spartan stadiu	871	0.47%	olin	2545	0.54%			
mp3,http://w\	853	0.46%	computer+sto	2292	0.48%			
michigan state	829	0.45%	chemistry	2048	0.43%			
maps	635	0.35%	cata	1981	0.42%			
michigan sta\	635	0.35%	spartan+trak	1904	0.40%			
honors college	542	0.30%	registrar	1832	0.39%			
michigan state	482	0.26%	payroll	1826	0.38%			
nursing	428	0.23%	stuinfo	1815	0.38%			
scopes trial	396	0.22%	human+resou	1741	0.37%			
how to write a	378	0.21%	housing	1636	0.34%			
michigan univ\	377	0.21%	lon+capa	1626	0.34%			
irgp	361	0.20%	jobs	1623	0.34%			
scopes monke	344	0.19%	wharton+cent	1591	0.33%			
margaret sand	344	0.19%	capa	1573	0.33%			
dupont analys	330	0.18%	athletics	1555	0.33%			
msu map	308	0.17%	im+east	1531	0.32%			
michigan state	266	0.14%	olin+health+c	1438	0.30%			
mp3,http://w\	262	0.14%	spartan+cash	1438	0.30%			
michigan state	257	0.14%	sparty+cash	1433	0.30%			
msu campus r	247	0.13%	schedule+of+\	1401	0.29%			
mp3,http://w\	223	0.12%	maps	1372	0.29%			
lyman briggs	220	0.12%	math	1370	0.29%			
michigan state	205	0.11%	college+of+ed	1342	0.28%			

FIGURE 5.10

Queries to the MSU.edu environment: Web-wide versus from the local search engine.

If you move farther down toward the long tail, you'll see even narrower queries. Today's narrow local search terms may be good predictors of tomorrow's valuable keywords, so use your more granular local queries to guide you on what keywords to bid on.

Going Beyond Sessions: Looking at Individual Searchers

If you can identify users, you will be able not only to identify their sessions, but also to learn more about them by looking at their information needs and search behaviors collectively. To demonstrate, I grabbed sets of queries from a few different TFANet searchers, dropped them into the wonderful word cloud tool wordle.net, and generated these clouds in Figures 5.11–5.13.

FIGURE 5.11
One TFANet's searcher's queries, rendered as a tag cloud...

FIGURE 5.12
...and another's...

FIGURE 5.13
...and another's.

While interesting curiosities by themselves, these single-user views can be incredibly powerful if they're representative of major audiences. That would enable you to incorporate search data into audience-related tools like personas. And personas based on actual data are more compelling than those that aren't.

But be careful: knowing who searched for what, while entirely fascinating, is nonetheless ethically fraught. That's what a set of AOL researchers learned—the hard way—when they innocently made AOL search data publicly available for research purposes.[3] Within hours, opportunistic busybodies grabbed the data set and threw it into query-able databases. Although the data did not include searchers' names, it *did* include user IDs. Which made it relatively simple to determine who—by name—was behind each user ID, as some enterprising *New York Times* reporters proved.[4] You obviously want to be careful with any kind of data that includes user IDs. In this book, I've focused on data and analysis that are typically more anonymous precisely for that reason.

Session analysis isn't for everyone, primarily because not every search engine or analytics application gathers this data. But if you do find a way to access it, I hope I've shown you the value of taking a closer look. Like all the other forms of analysis, session analysis—if nothing else—is yet another fantastic opportunity to dig deep into the search experience, and it will get you as close as you can to being inside the searcher's mind as she thinks her way through a single information need.

---

[3] The hard way, as in losing their jobs; read: http://en.wikipedia.org/wiki/AOL_search_data_scandal

[4] Read the story "A Face Is Exposed for AOL Searcher No. 4417749" from August 9, 2006: http://select.nytimes.com/gst/abstract.html?res=F10612FC345B0C7A8CDDA10894 DE404482 (login may be required).

Summary

- If you have access to information about *who* searched *what* and *when* on your site, conducting session analysis will help you gain deeper insight into what searchers do and how their needs change over a short period of time.

- Session analysis can provide more insight into what a searcher is actually trying to find; therefore, it's even better at revealing user intent than other forms of analysis.

- Session analysis helps you gain new perspective on why certain queries fail or why a weird query type keeps showing up in your logs.

- The best sessions to focus on include

  - Sessions that start and end with your most popular queries.

  - Sessions that end in failure (to fix them).

  - Sessions with specialized queries that are especially important to your business (such as product names).

- It's hard to define what exactly constitutes a search session. You'll have to be comfortable identifying a user need (query terms that qualitatively appear to belong together) and a set time range (for example, up to an hour).

- Be careful with user names and ID numbers; even the latter, when grouped, can reveal an individual's identity and risk violating that person's privacy.

CHAPTER 6

Audience Analysis

Why Segment Your Audience?   96
How to Segment Your Audience   99
Comparing and Contrasting Segments   104
What's Next?   106
Summary   107

Many people who are new to analytics—or who have managed to avoid it so far—are concerned that they'll be overwhelmed by the volume of data they'll be dealing with. That's a fair concern, especially if one is used to dealing with the far more manageable volume of data generated from, say, a 10-person user study. That's why I've encouraged you to begin your foray in SSA with a laser focus on the short head. It's a very manageable amount of data, and thanks to the Zipf Distribution, it goes a long way.

But there's another way to make the overwhelming, well...*whelming*: break your data into smaller segments based on audiences. You can then choose the most important audience to analyze, or prioritize, and work your way through each of them as time and resources allow. Either way, you'll get a more precise and nuanced view of user behavior, and you'll likely reduce the volume of data that you're analyzing.

Why Segment Your Audience?

Are all dog owners alike? It might seem that way to those uninitiated in canine ways. After all, what is there to owning a dog aside from walking it, feeding it, cleaning up after it, and giving it the occasional belly rub?

Well, Timmy and Wallace might disagree, as shown in Figure 6.1.

FIGURE 6.1
Not all dog owners are alike. Clearly. Just ask Lassie and Gromit.[1,2]

---

1   http://doggieaficionado.com/blog/wp-content/uploads/2009/10/lassie-and-timmy.jpg

2   www.winnipegfilmgroup.com/cinematheque/cabin_fever_the_incredible_adventures_of_wallace_and_gromit.aspx

While the Timmies and Wallaces of the world both love their dogs, they have very different reasons for owning them. Timmy looks to Lassie for guidance, love, and protection. Wallace sees Gromit as a partner in a daily routine built on a foundation of hijinks, inventions, and cheese. If you were designing for the segment of Wallace-like dog owners, your work would be drastically different than what you'd deliver for the Timmy segment.

Does your site's audience break out into segments as dramatically different as little boys and absent-minded inventors/bachelors? If it does, SSA will help you better understand how their information needs and searching experiences differ. If you're not sure, SSA will help you uncover what segments merit further consideration.

Aside from breaking down something big and untenable into more digestible parts, audience segmentation can help you in a variety of ways:

- **Assess which segments make sense—when you don't already know.** It's not always clear how to segment your users. For example, if your business is new, it may not have gotten to know its customers well enough to know which segments matter the most. Use pattern analysis (see Chapter 5, "Session Analysis") to get a better sense of the segments that might emerge simply from playing with your data. And use raw numbers—based upon the search traffic that each segment generates—to get a better sense of each segment's relative importance.

- **Beef up your personas.** If your organization already uses personas, perhaps it could do so more effectively if those personas were more grounded in data. Imagine injecting common information needs and tasks—derived from your site's queries—directly into your personas!

- **Tap into an existing culture of segmentation.** And if your organization is a true believer in audience segmentation, chances are it's still not incorporating site search query data into how it describes its segments. Another data point—especially one that so effectively describes each segment's information needs—will only improve your organization's ability to understand its audience segments. Conversely, you can sneakily establish SSA within your organization by piggybacking onto the existing segmentation analysis.

Not All Searchers Are Alike

Dog owners are not as alike as you might think. They want and need dogs for different reasons, and this is borne out through their queries.

Dogs as companions/best friends:

- Key needs/motivations: I want a dog to take on walks and to take me on walks. I live alone and have a dog to keep me company on activities like running, camping, hiking, exercising, and so on. The dog will help me get out more and meet people.

- Related search queries/tasks: dog runs, teaching dogs to catch frisbees, glasgow dog parks, meet-ups for dog owners, dog sitters.

Dogs as workers:

- Key needs/motivations: I need a dog to help me hunt/herd/rescue/sniff out drugs.

- Related search queries/tasks: field spaniel, fox hunt dogs, guard dog, search and rescue canine training, SAR dog training, police dog breeds.

Dogs as guides:

- Key needs/motivations: I need a dog to serve as my eyes.

- Related search queries/tasks: guide dogs london, training seeing-eye dogs, sponsor a guide dog, guide dogs in workplace.

Dogs as surrogate children:

- Key needs/motivations: I want a dog to shower with love and attention.

- Related search queries/tasks: LL Bean dog bed, liver doggie cookies, organic dog food, dog obedience school los angeles, dog airplane kennel, natural flea products.

Dogs as fashion accessories:

- Key needs/motivations: I want a dog to go with the rest of my outfit.

- Related search queries/tasks: toy chihuahua, dog sweater, doggie spa, rhinestone dog collar, puppy clothes.

- **Challenge the assumption that all your users are alike.** If you work at an organization that hasn't yet gotten UX religion, many of your colleagues—especially the ones who don't have direct contact with customers—may have a very imprecise picture of who your customers are. Or they may have a completely wrong one. Here's your chance to play with the data, see if some specific audiences emerge, and beat the naysayers about the head with real live data. Your ability to do so will, by the way, earn you many friends in both your marketing and product management groups.

How to Segment Your Audience

There are an almost infinite number of ways you can segment your users. Let's start with the easy ones first.

Segmenting the Easy Way

Some segmentation approaches are easy to work with because there's a good chance that your analytics application already supports some or all of them—like Google Analytics, for instance, as shown in Figure 6.2.

FIGURE 6.2

Google Analytics allows you to segment your queries in at least 25 ways.

Here are just some of those "easy" ways that you can likely segment your users by today:

- **Traffic sources:** In which domains did users' visits originate?

- **New versus repeat:** Are users first-time visitors, or have they been to your site before?

- **Loyalty:** How often do they visit?

- **Conversions:** Did or didn't they purchase the product? Or register for the workshop? Or complete the survey?

- **Average order or revenue per order:** How much money did they spend? As amounts live on a continuous scale, you'll want to set thresholds so you can create segments out of ranges (for example, $0.01–$9.99, $10.00–$24.99).

- **Geography:** Where are they located? How do such regions map to your sales territories?

- **Timing:** When do they make their purchases? As with order size, you'll have to set thresholds (for example, time of day, month, year).

Which segments should you check out? Consider what your organization is in business to do or what specific challenges it's facing at the moment. For example, if your business is struggling to succeed in the UK, it would be worth seeing if you can learn something about how the British searchers' information needs differ from those in other English-speaking markets. Or perhaps you want to understand the information needs of visitors who *don't* make a purchase on your site (versus those who do).

If your analytics application is kind enough to provide these segments, it's worth spending an hour or two experimenting with them. While the value of some will be obvious, others might surprise you. For example, what might you learn from analyzing common queries associated with different language segments?

In the example that follows, I've segmented one year's worth of queries from AIGA, the professional association for design, by language. It used

Google Analytics' pivot feature, selecting language, and was shown the top 10 most common queries, sorted by Total—all queries, regardless of language (see Figure 6.3). The Total column is followed by columns that break down the queries by specific languages:

- **en-us** means English speakers from the U.S.

- **en** means English speakers from other geographic areas.

- **es-es** means Spanish speakers from Spain.

- **en-gb** are English speakers from Great Britain.

- **pt-br** are Portuguese speakers from Brazil.

Pivot by: Language		Total	1. en-us	2. en	3. es-es	4. en-gb	5. pt-br
Search Term / None		Total Unique ↓ Searches	Total Unique Searches	Total Unique Searches	Total Unique Searches	Total Unique Searches	Total Unique Searches
1.	salary	1,737	1,584	125	6	0	0
2.	portfolio	1,256	1,130	97	0	6	0
3.	resume	1,214	1,081	104	0	27	0
4.	contract	1,039	976	20	13	0	6
5.	jobs	844	781	48	6	0	0
6.	salary survey	830	753	76	0	0	0
7.	symbols	830	544	0	125	13	20
8.	experience design	781	432	13	0	174	48
9.	cover letter	711	655	48	0	0	0
10.	graphic design	704	635	6	0	6	0

Showing: Total Unique Searches and (none)   1 - 5 of 69

Filter Search Term: containing   Go   Advanced Filter

FIGURE 6.3
AIGA's common queries segmented by language type. The default is set to Total—all languages combined—and subsequent columns show queries associated with 69 (!) language segments, starting with "en-us" (English speakers in the U.S.).

To start learning about common queries by language segment, I simply clicked that language's column. Here I've selected "en-us;" the top query is salary, followed by portfolio, and so on (see Figure 6.4).

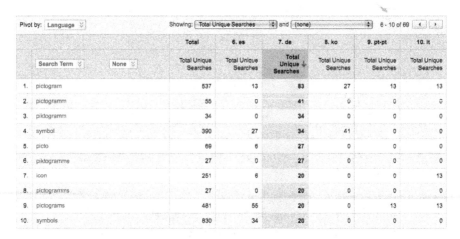

Pivot by: Language ⌄   Showing: [Total Unique Searches] and [(none)]   1 - 5 of 69 ◄ ►

Search Term ⌄ / None ⌄	Total Total Unique Searches	1. en-us Total Unique Searches	2. en Total Unique Searches	3. es-es Total Unique Searches	4. en-gb Total Unique Searches	5. pt-br Total Unique Searches
1. salary	1,737	1,584	125	6	0	0
2. portfolio	1,256	1,130	97	0	6	0
3. resume	1,214	1,081	104	0	27	0
4. contract	1,039	976	20	13	0	6
5. jobs	844	781	48	6	0	0
6. salary survey	830	753	76	0	0	0
7. cover letter	711	655	48	0	0	0
8. graphic design	711	642	6	0	6	0
9. internships	648	621	27	0	0	0
10. logo	704	572	27	13	6	6

Filter Search Term: [containing ⌄] [   ] Go   Advanced Filter

FIGURE 6.4

Common queries sorted by en-us—English speakers from the U.S. Eight of 10 seem to have something to do with employment.

Let's compare those Yankee queries with those from Germany. Interesting! Pictogram or variants thereof comprise 7 of the top 10 queries, as shown in Figure 6.5.

Pivot by: Language ⌄   Showing: [Total Unique Searches] and [(none)]   6 - 10 of 69 ◄ ►

Search Term ⌄ / None ⌄	Total Total Unique Searches	6. es Total Unique Searches	7. de Total Unique Searches	8. ko Total Unique Searches	9. pt-pt Total Unique Searches	10. it Total Unique Searches
1. pictogram	537	13	83	27	13	13
2. pictogramm	55	0	41	0	0	0
3. piktogramm	34	0	34	0	0	0
4. symbol	390	27	34	41	0	0
5. picto	69	6	27	0	0	0
6. piktogramme	27	0	27	0	0	0
7. icon	251	6	20	0	0	13
8. pictogramms	27	0	20	0	0	0
9. pictograms	481	55	20	0	13	13
10. symbols	830	34	20	0	0	0

FIGURE 6.5

Common queries sorted by "de." The Germans seem very interested in things that have something to do with pictograms.

Who knew that English-speaking Americans and Germans would have such different queries (and information needs)? I wouldn't have discovered this without a few minutes of "play" with the Google Analytics segmentation feature.

Now that I know *what* is interesting about these two segments, I need to decide whether it's important to know *why*. Should AIGA—a U.S.-based association—place great importance on reaching German speakers? Would it be useful to know why pictograms were so significant to German speakers? AIGA staff could follow up with a formal user study to learn why—or, at a minimum, they might simply float the question by their German colleagues. (They also might want to determine what percentage of their queries came from German speakers. If the portion were minimal, it might not be worth the effort to investigate further.)

Segmenting the Hard Way

It's nice to have ready-made segments like "language" available out of the box. But often the most interesting and useful segments are the ones that your analytics application knows nothing about: segments that are unique to your organization and its business model.

For example, your organization might want to classify users by where they are within the customer life cycle or by such demographics as age and income. If you're working with an intranet, your organization might find that segments based on employee role—administrator versus researcher versus customer support—would be the most useful. If you're running an annual conference, perhaps you'd like to know how first-time attendees' needs differ from those who have attended in past years. And as we've explored elsewhere in this book, you might find other time-based segments significant, like seasonality.

These segments are all clearly useful but require much more effort to obtain. It's likely you have the data you need *somewhere*—for example, you may be able to match employee roles with queries because employees have to log in to your intranet to search it, and you already know each employee's role. But having this sort of identifying data is one thing; integrating it with your query data is another, labor-intensive thing altogether. You may have to partner with the business units within your organization that own the data you need. Let's hope that your horse-trading skills are up to snuff, because that's what it might take to get the cooperation you need.

In fact, it's likely that the value of your segmentation approach is strongly correlated with the difficulty of obtaining the appropriate data. Can you justify the investment? As with so many things, it comes down to business value. But at least you now have a better idea of what kinds of questions are good candidates to invest in answering. And you have a model for how to proceed from our previous language segmentation example.

Comparing and Contrasting Segments

Let's jump into the nuts and bolts of using segmentation to analyze audiences.

The good news is that you can use all the analysis techniques that I've already covered in the book—pattern analysis, session analysis, and failure analysis—on your individual segments. You'll find that both seasonality and the Zipf Distribution also apply to your segments, and you'll likely start with each segment's short head before proceeding to its long tail.

And the bad news? There's none, really. The only major difference in audience analysis to note is that you can (and should) contrast and compare segments. Let's have a look at how the Open University, a distance learning-based academic institution in the United Kingdom, did just that.[3]

How Segments Differ

The Open University has three primary types of audiences: *enquirers* (users who've never logged into the site), *students* (users who can be identified as students by their login information), and *staff* (users who can be identified as staff by their login information). Examining the top 10 queries of each audience, the researchers found some significant differences between them, which are shown in Table 6.1.

---

3 This data and some of the analysis came from an unpublished paper on search behavior at the Open University (www3.open.ac.uk), written in 2007 by Caroline Jarrett, Whitney Quesenbery, Viki Stirling, and Sarah Allen.

TABLE 6.1

FREQUENT QUERIES AT THE OPEN UNIVERSITY		
Enquirers	Students	Staff
Psychology	exam results	jobs
Courses	short courses	library
Photography	credit transfer	ousa
Law	ousa	t171
Counseling	graduation	short courses
Nutrition	ousba	ousba
Social Work	library	credit transfer
Jobs	exam papers	s216
MBA	degree classification	openlearn
short courses	psychology	moodle

The top 10 queries for each of the Open University's three primary audiences.

From this minimal analysis, it's already apparent that enquirers are primarily focused on areas of study, such as psychology, photography, and law. That's not especially surprising. What is stunning is that photography and law *aren't taught at the Open University.* Such a finding might have great implications for the university's deans as they plan the institution's future. And it wouldn't have become apparent if the data hadn't been teased out into separate segments.

With such frequent queries as exam results, credit transfer, and graduation, students seem more focused on *finishing* their studies rather than the subjects themselves. Granted, this data had a very seasonal component; it was gathered during exam season, so it's not surprising that students should be fixating on a simpler, less stressful future without exams.

Course codes, like aa309 and dd304, already begin to appear within the top 25 of students' queries. Course codes also appear for staff, who often need to answer questions about specific courses; in such cases, they memorize course codes as mnemonics for quick lookup. Staff also frequently search for moodle, a content management system used by many academic institutions; since it's something they would likely navigate to, why are they searching for it? And, interestingly, the staff's top query is jobs; perhaps many staff are hoping to find positions for friends, checking their own job descriptions, or looking for an upgrade from their current positions.

Clearly, larger data samples and additional analysis will tell you more, especially long tail analysis, which will help you understand variations between segments in tone and types of content that are sought. But even each segment's top 10 queries exhibit very instructive differences and commonalities.

What's Next?

Once you have a better sense of which segments to study, how they differ, and what they share in common, you'll be positioned to apply other forms of site search analytics covered in this section of the book to those segments. Pattern analysis, for example, may help you understand how you might label content differently for different audiences. You might learn about where navigation fails by performing failure analysis on your segments. And segment analysis might show how their typical search experiences compare.

Like everything else, analyzing your data to learn about audience segments is an investment: the more you put into it, the more you'll get out of it. And the custom segments—the ones not necessarily supported by your analytics application—are likely to be the most valuable. But even if you stick to the easy segmentation approaches that may already be available to you, you'll learn something new.

Summary

- Audience analysis will help you better understand how information needs and searching experiences differ between audience segments.

- Challenge the assumption that your users are all alike. Even dog owners can be grouped into segments with very diverse needs and wants.

- Audience analysis can beef up your personas or boost your organization's existing segmentation analysis.

- A good way to start is to use the segments that your analytics application (for example, Google Analytics) may already offer. Then consider your organization's business model and build a few more of your own.

- Consider performing pattern analysis, session analysis, failure analysis, and goal-based analysis on each segment. See what they share in common and how they differ.

- Insights can help define what labels to use for various audiences, or types of content, to show or prioritize by role.

CHAPTER 7

Goal-Based Analysis

Goal Tracking Is Good, but Search Metrics
   Make It Better   110
Determining Goals and KPIs   113
Summary   119

E very organization has goals. Your organization is likely using conventional web analytics to measure how well its Web site or intranet is performing in helping it meet its business goals. But is it using metrics that come out of search?

If the answer's *no*, you're not alone. Lack of goal setting around (and involving) search is a chronic problem facing most organizations and a missed opportunity that can lead to loss of revenue.

The past four chapters showed you how to analyze your query data from the bottom up—so that useful insights would emerge. In this chapter, we'll take a *top-down* approach. We'll show you how SSA metrics can be a secret weapon in your organization's efforts to monitor, measure, and optimize site performance—to help you determine if your organization is on target to meet its business goals.

Goal Tracking Is Good, but Search Metrics Make It Better

Goals are nice, but if you're not tracking how well you're doing at meeting them, they're worthless. That's why KPIs (Key Performance Indicators) exist.[1] They force organizations to express and track their business goals in ways that are quantifiable and measurable.

From Goals to KPIs

For example, Central Michigan University developed a goal to improve its campus climate. While that sounds great, such a goal could end up as meaningless hand waving unless CMU makes this goal measurable and actually monitors how well it's doing at achieving that goal. How does one actually *know* that the campus climate is improving?

---

1 It's worth noting the difference between KPIs and metrics: metrics are simply measurements, while KPIs are metrics that map to organizational goals. Read Dennis Mortensen's brief article on the difference: http://visualrevenue.com/blog/2008/02/difference-between-kpi-and-metric.html

So CMU set out to create a KPI to measure campus climate.[2] Its KPI is based on measuring freshmen and seniors' *perceptions* of their campus climate, as determined by their responses to a short questionnaire. The questions specifically surveyed how much

1. Students asked questions, participated in class discussions, or both.

2. Students contributed to conversations with individuals different from themselves, in terms of religious beliefs, political opinions, or personal values.

3. Students spoke to faculty and staff regarding career plans.

CMU then set targets: it hoped to improve its scores over five years by 2.3% for freshmen and 2.1% for seniors. Now CMU had a measurable KPI that could help it determine how well it was doing at improving the campus climate over the course of several years. And, as the two charts in Figure 7.1 and 7.2 demonstrate, it's doing quite well.

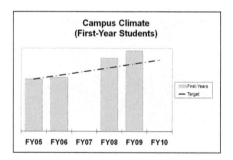

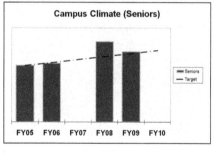

FIGURE 7.1
According to the target line, CMU seems on its way to meeting its goal of improving its campus climate for first-year students.

FIGURE 7.2
There was a drop in 2009 (and perhaps some missing data for 2007), but CMU's seniors are also enjoying an improved campus climate since the university began monitoring this KPI.

---

2 CMU was kind enough to share its KPI—and these charts—on its Web site: www.planning. cmich.edu/kpis.shtml

These KPIs are based on metrics that come from surveying students. It's a great start, but it's just one way to track how well things are going. And since no single type of user research is ideal, it's preferable to rely on multiple views of the same area (as we'll discuss in detail in Chapter 11, "Bridging Web Analytics and User Experience").

Souping Up a KPI with Search Metrics

What if CMU added another metric to the mix, one based on the volume of *search activity* related to the campus climate? Possible queries might include tracking the number of times students searched for, say, mental health-related content, which might be a good barometer for campus climate, and a target could be set for reducing those queries from one year to the next. CMU could track changes in the annual volume of searches for such terms as mental health, counseling, therapy, psychologist, emotional health, and depression, hoping to see these keyword searches decline year after year. The data might look like Figure 7.3 when charted.

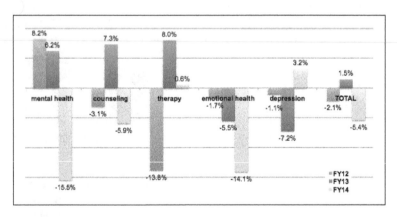

FIGURE 7.3
Year-to-year changes in the volume of mental health-related queries; fortunately, the volume of queries is decreasing.

This hypothetical chart shows the percentage change from year to year for each query and for all the queries (tallied up as "Total"). From the search data, you could conclude that the drop in searches related to mental health matters could support survey data that the campus climate was improving. CMU could use the Total as an additional metric—along with survey responses—to help measure the KPI of campus climate.

Analyzing query data is less expensive than designing, running, gathering, and analyzing the many results from a series of annual surveys—and less expensive to learn from. Using both forms of user research leads to a KPI that's more robust than one that relies on a single, imperfect source of data to measure. And therein lies the opportunity: organizations can really benefit if they would augment their goal-tracking efforts with the data gleaned from site search analytics. I'll show you how to do it.

Determining Goals and KPIs

Let's face it, I can't tell you what the goals of your organization and its site are or should be. If you don't know, you should start talking with as senior a manager as you can find immediately.

But I can tell you that your organization's site is likely to match at least one of four main types: commerce, content, lead generation, or self-service support sites. I'll briefly describe each type in the sections that follow, so familiarizing yourself with them will help you get a better grasp of your site's goals and their corresponding KPIs. Once you have a better sense of your KPIs, you'll find it easier to determine how to fold search metrics into them.

Four Main Types of Organizational Sites

- **Commerce sites, like Amazon and eBay.** Their primary goal is to get customers to buy their products or services. For such sites, search is probably more critical than in any other type of site, as many customers arrive at their sites knowing what they want to purchase. A typical commerce site KPI might be "To increase sales among customers in emerging markets." To enrich that KPI, you might incorporate a search metric like "Percentage of conversion rates of top 20 most common queries for product names" into it.

- **Content-rich sites, like ESPN, the *New York Times*, and YouTube.** The goal of these sites is to entertain or enrich users with content—to read, watch, play, learn from, and enjoy. Such sites typically generate income in two ways:

  - **Ad Service:** These sites sell ad space on their pages and make money every time an ad is served or clicked through. An ad service-related KPI may be "Increase the amount of time spent on the site." A supporting search metric could be "Average time spent on site after searching."

  - **Subscription:** A subscription is essentially a type of purchase, so these types of sites share much in common with commerce sites. A subscription KPI could simply be "Increase the rate at which subscribers renew." A relevant search metric could be "# search traffic originating from within the subscription process."

- **Lead generation sites, like LendingTree.com and SelectQuote.com.** The goal of these sites is to capture personally identifiable information about your site's visitors so you can follow up with them later. This can include traditional offline transactions or customer relationship management (CRM) efforts. A lead generation KPI could be "Convert more leads into prospects," and a supporting search metric could be "Conversion ratio of visitors who use site search."

- **Self-service/support sites, like Microsoft Support, GetSatisfaction.com.** Their goal is to save you money: visitors use your Web site to solve any issues, instead of utilizing costly alternatives, such as call centers. A possible KPI: "Reduce call center support tickets"; a supporting search metric: "Volume of traffic for such support-related queries as 'support,' 'technical support,' 'help,'" and so on.

The first three types of sites bring in money; the last one saves money (by reducing an organization's expenses). Either way, it's about the money. And just about every organization's site in the world can be said to follow at least two of these models.

Once you have a sense of your organization's goals and the KPIs that correspond with them, you can begin determining metrics that help you measure those KPIs. So, just as Central Michigan University can monitor its KPI of campus climate by measuring student survey responses (and, as I suggested, searches for mental health-related content), you can develop your own metrics to power your KPIs. To get a deeper understanding of KPIs, as well as a zillion great examples, I recommend Eric T. Peterson's wonderful *The Big Book of Key Performance Indicators* and Avinash Kaushik's *Web Analytics: An Hour a Day*.

Search Metrics Based on Query Data

For now, let's turn to covering some *search metrics* that you can use to beef up your KPIs or use as KPIs. The following set of search metrics in Table 7.1 was graciously provided by analytics whiz Marko Hurst. The list is by no means comprehensive, but if you think of it like a menu, these metrics should be very useful for you to consider as you integrate search into measuring your site's performance. Please note that while most are based on query data, some will require server log data as well.

TABLE 7.1

SEARCH METRICS FROM MARKO HURST		
Search Metric	Purpose	Notes
% queries that retrieve zero results	Measures the quality of your search results, based on the degree to which your search results are failing. Typically used as a KPI.	Zero queries generally mean failure, so your goal should be to make this number as small as possible. Exception is when users are simply trying to validate that a piece of content does not exist. For example, they search Network Solutions for a domain name they want to buy, and hopefully, no one has taken it.
% queries where users click on a search result	Measures the quality of your search results based on the degree your results are being clicked on by users. Typically used as a KPI.	If a search result is clicked, it's likely that it's at least interesting and engaging, even if irrelevant. So no clicks may mean poor results. You don't need this metric if users can find what they need by scanning search results, rather than clicking through. For example, if they are searching for a colleague's phone number in a staff directory, they may see it within the search result. No click needed.

continues on next page

TABLE 7.1 *continued*

SEARCH METRICS FROM MARKO HURST		
Search Metric	Purpose	Notes
% queries that lead to users exiting the site (aka search bounce rate or search exit rate)	Measures the quality of the overall search experience based on the degree users leave without clicking on any results. Typically used as a KPI.	When users immediately leave your site after searching, it can be inferred that their expectations were not met. It may have been due to a poor search interface, irrelevant results, or some other search-related factor.
% sessions that use search	Compares the usage of your site's search system versus browsing. Can be used as a KPI or metric.	Knowing the degree to which users rely upon search helps determine how much you should invest in developing and improving your search system.
Average # queries per session	Tracks how frequently users search during a single session. Typically used as a metric.	Most useful when cross-referenced with specific keywords that are being used within a single session (see *Search Refinement Rate*). If the queries are duplicates or synonyms, users may be flailing, indicating poor search performance.
Average # search result pages viewed per query	Measures the quality of your search results. Typically used as a metric.	If the number is greater than one, users may not be finding the most relevant results on the first page. Keep in mind that this measures the performance of individual queries, rather than your site overall.
Average # pages viewed after searching	Measures the quality of your site's content and calls to action. Typically used as a metric.	The act of searching itself is only a step in the process. What did users do after they searched? Did they take the action you hoped they would? Compare this metric with *Average # pages viewed before searching*.
Average time spent on site after searching	Measures users' level of engagement and satisfaction after search. Typically used as a metric.	The more time users spend on your site is often—though not always—a good indicator of their satisfaction level. Temper this assumption by cross-referencing this metric with others, such as *Average # pages viewed after searching* and *Goal/conversion completion rate*.
Average time spent on site before searching	Measures the effectiveness of your site's navigation. Typically used as a metric.	Often users will use search when they become frustrated; knowing what that threshold is can help inform your design decisions. Compare this metric with *Average time on site without search* in conjunction with *Goal/conversion completion rate*.
Average time spent on each search results page	Measures the usability of your site's search engine results pages. Typically used as a metric.	Longer times might be an indicator that your SERP design is confusing or contains too much information. Follow this metric over time to see if it goes up or down in response to your design tweaks.

TABLE 7.1 *continued*

SEARCH METRICS FROM MARKO HURST		
Search Metric	Purpose	Notes
Conversion ratio of visitors who use site search	Measures the quality of the overall search experience, compared to those who browsed. Typically used as a KPI.	This is another way to look at how well your site's search is performing compared with its browsing experience.
Average # items added from search results	Measures the number of items marked or added to a cart after using search. Typically used as a metric.	Applicable for sites that have a shopping cart or similar "basket" functionality. Use in conjunction with other metrics, such as *Search conversion rate, Top search terms with corresponding conversion rates,* and *Average time spent on site after searching* to make a case for greater investment in your system.
Session duration for all sessions that included searches	Measures the average time spent on your site for users that searched. Typically used as a metric.	Compare with *Session duration for all sessions that didn't include search* to get a good sense of whether users are exploring more or less with search than with browsing. Considering your site's goals, is this a good thing?
Search conversion rate	Measures the overall percentage of searches that result in a conversion. Used as both a KPI or a metric.	Helps determine how many users "converted" using search. The term *conversion* can go beyond making purchases; conversions can also include downloading, signing up, registering, and other actions.
Search refinement rate	Measures the quality and relevancy of search engine results pages related to a user query. Typically used as a KPI.	High rates of refinement typically mean that the SERPs did not meet the users' expectations and that users are continuing to seek results despite their poor experience.
Most frequent search terms	Tracks the most commonly searched queries. Typically used as a metric.	You should know your top queries by heart, as they are the most popular and, likely, the most valuable to your site's users.
Most frequent queries with corresponding conversion rates	Tracks the overall performance of your most common queries. Typically used as a KPI.	The term *conversion* can go beyond making purchases; conversions can also include downloading, signing up, registering, and other actions. Follow these queries over time to understand your users' needs, especially queries that are frequently searched and evergreen.
Most frequent pages on the site where site search was initiated	Tracks the quality of content, design, and page (CMS) templates. Used as both a KPI or a metric.	Shows where users became frustrated with content or navigation and decided to begin searching. Learn more by determining if these pages are related. Do they share the same design? Or CMS template? Note that if search is the user's *first* action on the site, it should not be included in this metric.

continues on next page

TABLE 7.1 *continued*

SEARCH METRICS FROM MARKO HURST		
Search Metric	Purpose	Notes
Total # of unique searches	Measures the breadth and depth of your users' natural language. Typically used as a metric.	By itself, this list doesn't mean a lot to very many people, but when it is broken down and examined, it's probably the most valuable list you will come across because it is your users' confessions of what they are trying to find in their own words. This is a gold mine of data that can be directly applied to your keywords, metadata, SEO, SEM, navigation, ontology, taxonomy, page titles, ‹h› tags, etc. This is invaluable data to apply for greater findability, accessibility, and relevancy.

Marko Hurst's list of search metrics. Not exhaustive, but quite useful!

More and more organizations invest heavily in KPIs for measuring site performance. But so many continue to completely forgo incorporating search metrics into their performance analysis. Perhaps it's simply too new or too strange for them to consider. We hope this list of search metrics helps you change all that for your organization.

From Top-Down to Bottom-Up Analysis

Goal-based analysis (or top-down analysis) is a critical component of site search analytics (and, really, any type of analytics). You start with clear goals—expressed as KPI—that come from the upper levels of your organization's management. Therefore, you know that, by benchmarking, measuring, and monitoring performance, you're getting a better read of what's important to your organization. In effect, goal-based analysis gives you a better sense of how well your organization's site is performing in the *world that you know.* When it is combined with the emergent, less-quantitative analysis methods we covered in the prior four chapters— which, in effect, teach you about the patterns, trends, and surprises that make up the world that *you don't know*—you'll have a powerful, balanced toolkit to gain incredible insights from your query data.

Summary

- Search metrics—many of which come straight from query analysis—can be a secret weapon in your organization's efforts to monitor, measure, and optimize site performance—to help you determine if your organization is on target to meet its business goals.

- Many Key Performance Indicators (KPIs) are missing search-related metrics; here's your chance to fix that.

- Start by understanding your organization's business model, which typically falls into at least one of these four main types:

  - Commerce sites

  - Content-rich sites

  - Lead generation sites

  - Self-serve or support sites

- Start with clear goals and corresponding KPIs around your site that come from the upper management of your organization. This gives you key benchmarking targets to use to measure and monitor site performance.

- Use your site goals and KPIs as critical context for selecting relevant search metrics from the menu found in this chapter. Plug in, play, measure, analyze, and improve. Repeat.

CHAPTER 8

Practical Tips for Improving Search

Plugging Gaps in Your Search Engine's Index   122

Making Query Entry Easier by Fixing "the Box"   122

Accommodating Strange Query Syntax   124

Determining What Your Best Bets Should Be   126

Helping Searchers Auto-Complete Their Queries   127

Improving a "No Results Found" Page   129

Helping Searchers Revise Their Queries to Get
   Better Results   130

Designing Search Results Around Specialized
   Query Types   132

Designing Search Results Around Specialized
   Content Types   137

Summary   142

T he previous five chapters gave you some techniques to use to analyze and act upon your query data. In the next three chapters, I'll show you some specific benefits that come directly from site search analytics, starting with improving your site's search system.

Plugging Gaps in Your Search Engine's Index

It's a dirty little secret that search engines don't always index all the content they're supposed to. The problem isn't with the software itself. Rather, it's due to the engine simply not knowing about content areas that exist on a given site. And the engine may not know because it's likely that *you* don't. If your site is actually a large set of subsites—typical of many enterprise-scale Web environments—then it's simply hard to know what content is out there.

One solution is to analyze your top queries with zero results. Of those, identify which aren't retrieving results because there simply *is no content* to match searchers' needs.

Then look at those queries as a group. First, are you surprised by what you find? Do you see any patterns, anything in common at all? Would you have expected there to be content to match those queries? If so, who would have created it, and in what unit would they likely work?

You're mostly there, Holmes; now go talk to someone in that part of your organization. Find out if there is, indeed, content that needs to be crawled in order to match these null queries (and if not, to make a gentle recommendation that it should be created).

Making Query Entry Easier by Fixing "the Box"

Most sites these days happily sport "the box," a simple text-entry box (and an accompanying "search" button) that persists on every page in a fixed position (see Figure 8.1). It's a life preserver of sorts—searchers know exactly where to look for it when they need to execute a search, and it works the same way wherever they find it.

FIGURE 8.1

Even a Web environment as large as IBM.com has a persistent simple search entry box.

If you have "the box" in place throughout your site, congratulations! But have you considered how wide it should be? It had better be wide enough to accommodate the majority of your queries. SSA will help you figure out how long your queries typically run, so you can plan your design of the text-entry box accordingly.

In this example, I analyzed AIGA's top 500 unique queries for a specific month—these accounted for exactly 37% of all search activity (see Figure 8.2). I used Microsoft's "LEN" function to count the number of characters in each query and then calculated the queries' mean and median lengths (10.648 and 10, respectively).

Query	Query Count	Query %	Cumulative %	Query Length	Mean Length
salary	152	1.44%	1.44%	6	10.648
contract	86	0.81%	2.25%	8	
salary survey	73	0.69%	2.94%	13	Median Length
cover letter	66	0.62%	3.57%	12	10
experience design	64	0.61%	4.18%	17	
jobs	64	0.61%	4.78%	4	
resume	61	0.58%	5.36%	6	
portfolio	54	0.51%	5.87%	9	
pricing	49	0.46%	6.33%	7	
symbols	44	0.42%	6.75%	7	
freelance	41	0.39%	7.14%	9	
logo	38	0.36%	7.50%	4	
conference	37	0.35%	7.85%	10	
web design	34	0.32%	8.17%	10	
pictogram	33	0.31%	8.48%	9	
apple discount	32	0.30%	8.79%	14	
salaries	32	0.30%	9.09%	8	
typography	31	0.29%	9.38%	10	
internships	30	0.28%	9.67%	11	
contracts	30	0.28%	9.95%	9	
book design	27	0.26%	10.21%	11	
icons	27	0.26%	10.46%	5	
portfolios	26	0.25%	10.71%	10	
books	25	0.24%	10.95%	5	
cover letters	23	0.22%	11.16%	13	
freelance rates	22	0.21%	11.37%	15	

FIGURE 8.2

The most frequent AIGA.org queries—and their lengths.

After I sorted by query length, you can see that the maximum length among these 500 queries was 62 characters, but that is something of an outlier; the next longest was 36, then 28, and then it flattened out (apparently, Zipf is everywhere), as shown in Figure 8.3.

Query Length
62
36
28
26
25
25
25
23
22
22

FIGURE 8.3

The short head of AIGA's queries by length; notice the quick drop-off.

Based on this data, I might be safe using a search entry box with a width in the 15–20 character range. If horizontal real estate isn't at a premium, a width of 30 characters would be even better.

I could take my analysis further and compare a sample from the long tail and see if query length differs greatly. Still, with this small sample, I'm safely addressing our most frequent queries and almost 40% of all search activity.

Accommodating Strange Query Syntax

Once upon a time, prior to the advent of the Web, most online searching was done in either library catalogs or commercial databases that were hugely expensive to use (think hundreds of dollars by the hour) and usually horribly designed. Accordingly, searchers in those days were more than casual and definitely not lazy. They were quite motivated to learn all sorts of search tricks, like using Boolean operators (for example, OR, AND, and NOT), wildcards, ways to truncate terms, and lots of other weirdness.

These days, Google is good enough that most searchers can be lazy, entering a term or two, and expecting something reasonably good in return. Still, there are a few holdouts, and if your site is older or tends to be used by researchers or librarians, there's a good chance that you may need to consider supporting old-style query syntax.

A simple way to check is to search your queries for such instances. In the example below, I used Google Analytics to filter a year's worth of *AIGA. org* queries for the operator OR (see Figure 8.4). Of the over 75,000 unique queries for the entire year, only 121 unique queries (and 142 searches overall) included OR. And most of those queries were *not* using OR as a Boolean operator.

	Search Term ⌄	None ⌄	Total Unique ↓ Searches
1.	mac or pc		4
2.	to design or not to design		4
3.	to spec or not to spec		4
4.	To spec or not to spec		3
5.	visual or verbal		3
6.	To Design or Not to Design: A Conversation with		2
7.	What's in a Name: The History of Graphic Desig		2
8.	Writing 101: Visual or Verbal?		2
9.	X for All or Nothing		2
10.	design and the bottom line or business		2
11.	portfolio or book		2
12.	work experience or graphic design degree		2
13.	x for all or nothing		2

FIGURE 8.4
AIGA's searchers aren't using the Boolean OR operator very often.

The use of AND, however, was a bit more common; it was included in 1,596 unique queries and 2,205 searches overall. (NOT showed up in 84 unique queries and 112 searches overall.) But out of over 75,000 unique queries and 188,000 searches overall, the volume of searching using Boolean queries is still quite small—in the 1%–2% range—and the majority of those queries *don't* use AND, OR, and NOT as Boolean operators. So AIGA is probably safe in not supporting Boolean operators in its query syntax.

Determining What Your Best Bets Should Be

Best bets (aka "recommended links") are simple. They're search results that have been manually connected to a particular query. Why do this? Because search engines are robots, and robots aren't always that effective at retrieving good search results.

In the example in Figure 8.5, the National Cancer Institute wanted to make sure that searchers always retrieved something useful when searching for melanoma. The organization manually attached three sets of best bet search results to the query, and these are displayed *before* the search engine's automated results show up.

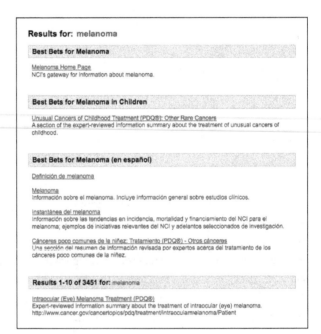

FIGURE 8.5
When searching cancer.gov for melanoma, you'll find best bet search results front and center.

So, while best bets are simple, they're also powerful. "Powerful" in the sense that they can really improve the search experience. And "powerful" in that they can be a weapon wielded in your organization's political battles.

For example, who gets to determine which are the most appropriate best bets for a query? If, for example, your organization sells hardware products, and someone searches for a product's name, should there be a best bet result from marketing? Or from sales? Or from the tech support department? Whose should be the highest priority? This sort of situation can spin out into a political firefight very quickly.

And who gets to determine which queries merit best bets in the first place? (And how many should there be at most? We've not seen this addressed by researchers, but three or four seems plenty, since you don't want to completely obstruct the raw search results.)

Rather than let best bets become a political headache, use data—query data—to quell or at least blunt these battles. Look to the short head for common queries, and look at them longitudinally to determine which are the most persistent over time. The combination of *popularity* and *persistence* is a great driver for choosing queries that merit best bets.

If you do have multiple best bet candidates, consider prioritizing them by determining the relative importance of a particular query to different audience segments. Consider our hardware vendor once more: if the people searching a specific product name are three times more likely to be existing customers seeking to download drivers, rather than prospects who might be looking to learn about a product, then the data would suggest that tech support's best bet should come first. Argument settled.

Helping Searchers Auto-Complete Their Queries

Unless you've been under a rock for the past few years, you've likely encountered sites that automatically complete your queries (also known as "type-ahead"). In effect, the search engine has been given enough information to predict what you want to search—or, at least, provide you with a few useful possibilities for you to select from. Auto-completion can help searchers save time entering a query. They can just click or tab over to their selection, rather than continue typing. And if they're not exactly sure how to enter their query—perhaps they don't know the proper spelling of a term—auto-completion will expose some useful possibilities.

Where does SSA fit in auto-completion? Well, it might be tempting to simply use all of your queries—or even your most frequent queries—as your auto-completion list, but beware: these queries are likely to be quite dirty in all senses. They'll include typos, irrelevant terms, and terms that are dirty in the pornographic sense.

Rather than using raw queries, rely on a cleaned-up version. For example, you may already have a list of keywords associated with best bet search results. Given that they're probably based on your frequent queries and that they've been scrubbed, they're a great starting point. You might also consider using a tool that can perform entity extraction on your queries to give you a set of proper nouns for your auto-completion list. But again, you'll still need to manually review such a list; no software application will be able to do that as well as you can.

SSA can also help you identify metadata attributes and content types (see Chapter 3, "Pattern Analysis"). Consider them candidates for items to add to an auto-completion list. You may find that you can go out and acquire certain metadata—say, place names—from commercial sources and insert them directly into your auto-completion list. (Just make sure that your newly added terms have content associated with them, or they'll be navigational dead-ends.) Or you may already have the terms you need somewhere inside your organization.

For example, ESPN.com enables searchers to type ahead and retrieve names of professional athletes, as shown in Figure 8.6.

FIGURE 8.6
Auto-completion of players' names at ESPN.com.

Improving a "No Results Found" Page

Whoever issued the click that led to the following page in Figure 8.7 should be reported to the authorities immediately. Bad user!

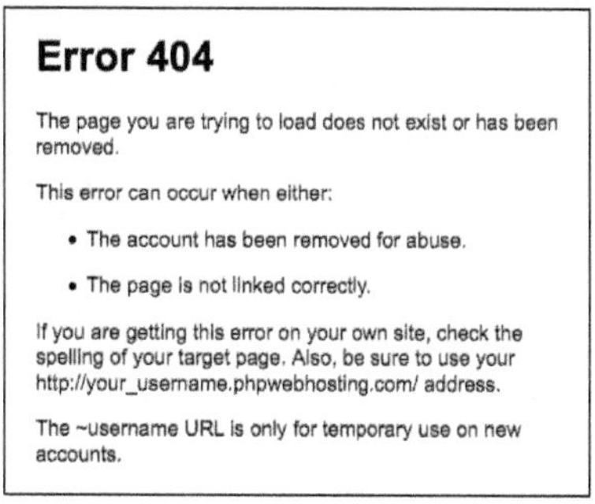

Error 404

The page you are trying to load does not exist or has been removed.

This error can occur when either:

- The account has been removed for abuse.
- The page is not linked correctly.

If you are getting this error on your own site, check the spelling of your target page. Also, be sure to use your http://your_username.phpwebhosting.com/ address.

The ~username URL is only for temporary use on new accounts.

FIGURE 8.7
Shame on you! (from http://astro.phpwebhosting.com/404.html).

We've all seen error messages like these before. Some are unhelpful (see Figure 8.7), while others seem to go out of their way to make you feel like a lunkhead. Many sites are addressing their messaging of their "file not found" pages, moving from 404-impersonality to a more helpful approach that suggests alternatives.

Similarly, there's no reason not to go beyond default "results not found" pages and do even better. And SSA can help in a very simple way, as shown in Figure 8.8.

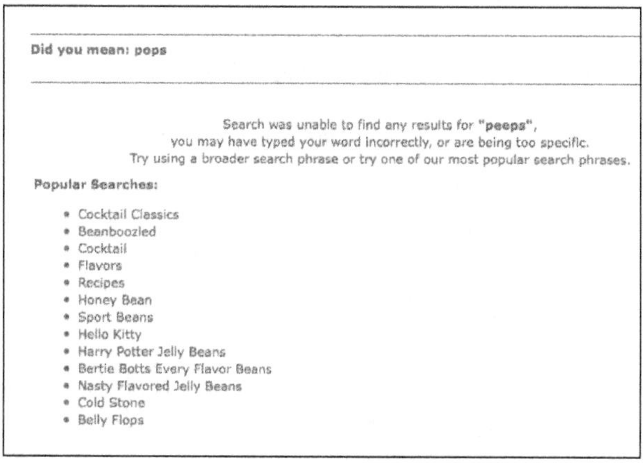

Did you mean: pops

Search was unable to find any results for **"peeps"**, you may have typed your word incorrectly, or are being too specific. Try using a broader search phrase or try one of our most popular search phrases.

Popular Searches:

- Cocktail Classics
- Beanboozled
- Cocktail
- Flavors
- Recipes
- Honey Bean
- Sport Beans
- Hello Kitty
- Harry Potter Jelly Beans
- Bertie Botts Every Flavor Beans
- Nasty Flavored Jelly Beans
- Cold Stone
- Belly Flops

FIGURE 8.8
No "peeps" at the JellyBelly.com site? No worries; help is on the way.

Certainly, *JellyBelly.com*'s copy could be even a tad bit more helpful. But more importantly, the company realizes that, in the context of a failed search, it's a good idea to suggest other queries to try. These suggestions are frequent queries; even better would be suggesting queries with synonyms for the failed query term. (But let's face it: there probably are no synonyms for "peeps.") Either way, the searcher is now just one click away from more search results, rather than being made to feel like an idiot.

Helping Searchers Revise Their Queries to Get Better Results

As searchers get past the initial query entry interface and start to encounter search results pages, they become increasingly likely to invest more effort into finding what they need. There are many reasons for this—the scent of desired information may be getting stronger;[1] they don't luck out into great results the first go-round as they'd hoped; or they learn more about what they're looking for as they engage with search results. Whatever the case may be, this is a good time to expose them to a higher level of search functionality that is afforded by the common starting point of "the Box."

It's likely that your search engine already has many great features to help searchers revise their queries and massage their search results. Unfortunately, it's also likely that these features have been buried in a search system's sad ghetto, infamously known as *Advanced Search*. (Did you know that "Advanced Search" is actually search engine vendor terminology for a "Miscellaneous bucket of features that we don't know what you'll do with [but we wish you the best of luck]?")

Like any other kind of help feature, these types of search features work best when presented within the appropriate context of use. Your search engine vendor can't or won't help you figure out which of these features to provide to searchers and when, so it's up to you to do the heavy lifting. Fortunately, SSA (and a little common sense) can help.

---

1   For more on the "scent of information," read Peter Pirolli and Stuart Card's "Information Foraging" in *Psychology Review*; 1999, Vol. 106, No. 4 (pp.643-675).

Two of the most common motivations for revising a search have to do with adjusting the volume of results—either the engine isn't returning enough, or it's returning too many. In the first case, you can guess that a null results page is too few—or you might set your threshold a little higher—say, five results. In the latter case, you might set a threshold of more than one or two screenfuls of results, because you're fairly certain searchers won't get past those initial sets of results.

In either case, look to integrate features from your Advanced Search interface that broaden or narrow, respectively. For example, the University of Alaska Fairbanks' Advanced Search interface consists exclusively of a means for broadening your search results, as shown in Figure 8.9.

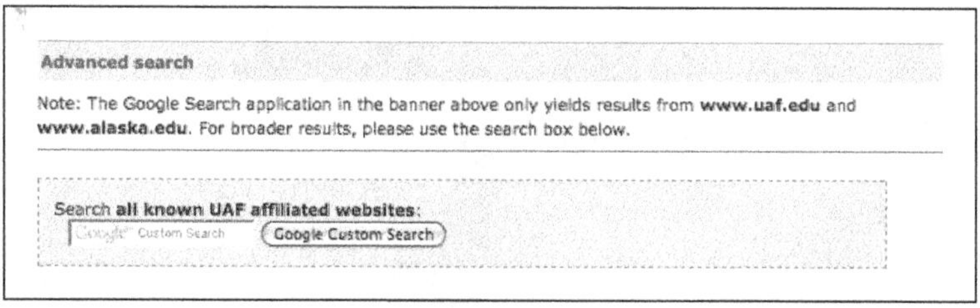

Advanced search

Note: The Google Search application in the banner above only yields results from **www.uaf.edu** and **www.alaska.edu**. For broader results, please use the search box below.

Search **all known UAF affiliated websites**:

Google Custom Search (Google Custom Search)

FIGURE 8.9
At the University of Alaska Fairbanks, Advanced Search means "broaden your search." Why not expose these features when the search results need expanding? (www.uaf.edu/uaf/search)

The IRS, on the other hand, provides all sorts of ways to narrow a search from its Advanced Search interface (see Figure 8.10).

Clearly, Advanced Search means different things to different people. Rather than relying on that term having any sort of consistent meaning, consider simply designing your search results pages to incorporate whatever form of refinement *made sense* given the situation: support expanded results if zero were retrieved, or ways to narrow results if too many were retrieved. This approach would likely be much more helpful than burying such features on an Advanced Search page.

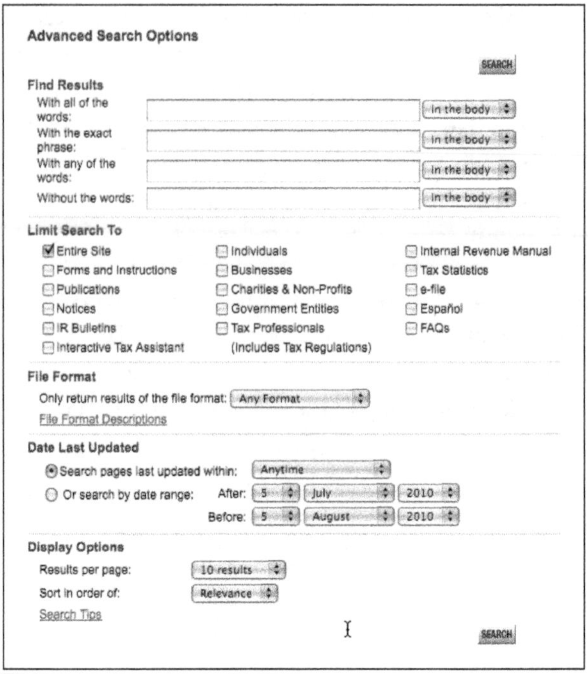

FIGURE 8.10
At the IRS, Advanced Search means "narrow your search." (http://search.irs.gov/web/advanced-search.htm)

Designing Search Results Around Specialized Query Types

Certain query types are worth looking for as you dig into your query data, especially your long tail, because you can tune how your results are presented and how they can be sorted. Specialized types of queries may include such search terms as

- Unique identification numbers, such as ISBNs, SKUs, and course codes

- Proper nouns (names of people, places, or objects)

- Acronyms

- Dates

- Navigational queries (URLs)

Search Pre-Refinement: How Much Customization to Allow

Gary Angel, President, Semphonic—http://semphonic.com

For most sites, the simpler the search interface you offer, the better. Thanks to Google, searchers are deeply familiar with basic keyword searching methods and can use them effectively. Advanced Search tools don't usually work any better, and, if poorly conceived, often work rather worse than basic keyword search. There are important exceptions, however, where encouraging searchers to provide additional criteria for their initial search makes good sense.

For sites where search is the almost universal method of finding things, especially where faceting is necessary, providing up-front search refinement makes good sense. If you manage a hotel site, an airline site, or a real estate site, then form-based (aka advanced) search is far more efficient than keyword search.

For example, in real estate sites nearly all searches begin with a city name. For the vast majority of searchers, however, a citywide search—regardless of how the results are sorted—will return too many results to be used effectively. The results should be faceted by price, neighborhood, or categories like size or number of bedrooms. Airlines face a similar search problem. Almost every search begins with both a date and, at minimum, a trip leg (a from: to pair), as shown in Figure 8.11. The same is true for almost any travel application, including hotel and car rental sites.

FIGURE 8.11
A single field search box wouldn't make sense for travel sites like Expedia.com.

continues on next page

Search Pre-Refinement: How Much Customization to Allow (continued)

For most industries, there is a fairly obvious subjective ordering of at least a few primary fields. As with most subjective orderings, however, there are always questions. For example, we may know that far more people will search a real estate site based on price or neighborhood than, say, pools. You don't need analytics to tell you that. But not every question is quite so obvious. For home search, is price or neighborhood more important? Is number of bedrooms or bathrooms more important? Or do you need both? What about square feet?

The goal of analytics is to help answer, or give the necessary information to answer, questions like these. If you start with the assumption that the fewer choices you give searchers, the cleaner and better the interface, how do you decide how many choices and which choices are best?

In general, the goal of search refinement is to narrow the range of search results to some optimum level. You can test facet combinations on initial search relative to two different criteria:

- Number of search results produced

- Search outcomes (measured either by product detail views or conversion results)

In the real estate case shown in Figure 8.12, "Pct of Searches Used" captures how often visitors actually used a field when submitting a search. "Lift" measures whether visitors who searched using a field were more or less likely to submit a lead. Four fields (Neighborhood, Property Type, Square Feet, and Amenities) all showed negative lift— meaning visitors using these features were less likely to submit a lead than users who did not. In other words, on average they decreased the effectiveness of search when included in the initial search.

You'll also note that Bedrooms and Bathrooms and Maximum Price worked very well as fields for an initial search. The bottom line is that analysis of the lift and number of results returned based on the initial search make it much easier to make intelligent decisions about how many and which options are worth providing to searchers.

Search Pre-Refinement: How Much Customization to Allow (continued)

Sub-Selection	Pct of Searches Used	Lift
Max. Price	26.3%	4.9%
Min. Price	18.6%	1.1%
Neighborhood	24.8%	-2.1%
Bedrooms	13.8%	7.2%
Bathrooms	10.0%	8.4%
Property Type	13.0%	-1.8%
MLS	8.7%	8.3%
Keyword	2.7%	0.9%
Square Feet	1.3%	-2.0%
Amenities	1.1%	-5.3%

FIGURE 8.12
The data suggests that the presence of fields like "Neighborhood" in a form decrease the search's effectiveness.

In every case for this study, the least effective fielded searches produced, on average, very small result sets. That won't always be the case. There is no single right answer to an optimal number of search results returned, particularly across different problem sets. People need to see more search results for houses than they would for kitchen blenders. The critical factor is the degree to which the search criteria can reliably identify what the visitor is looking for. Housing search is necessarily fairly fuzzy.

If unique IDs are usual suspects within your query data, you may be able to program your search engine to look for them—their syntax is usually consistent and predicable—and present custom search results for that specific type of query. So a commerce site might recognize a search for 0-38533-349-8 to be for a book's ISBN, and would accordingly know to display a cover thumbnail and other information to help the searcher identify and purchase Kurt Vonnegut's *The Sirens of Titan*.

A person's name might work the same way, although name recognition isn't as surefire as unique IDs. For example, you might teach your search engine to flag a mixed case string of two words separated by a comma (for example, Vonnegut, Kurt) as a name. You could also define a person's name more loosely, such as a string of any two words in mixed case (for example, Kurt Vonnegut, but also Chopped Liver). The latter case has its obvious drawbacks, but could still be workable if your search engine is searching a federated collection of data stores. In such a case, you could have it default to display results from the staff directory first. If there is no one with the name "Chopped Liver" in your staff directory, your search engine could move on and grab results from elsewhere (like your intranet's extensive collection of lunchroom menus).

Place names, organization names, and acronyms are often already known. For example, you can purchase or steal lists of place names (or in some cases, like U.S. states, cull them from your memory). Your organization may have lists of its internal division names and its partners' names. And it may also maintain a glossary of acronyms (which, by the way, you can grow from analyzing queries if you need to). If so, you can feed these to your search engine in advance and provide well-crafted search results using the same approach as you would for best bets.

Dates (and, less frequently, place names) are helpful in a slightly different way—rather than helping identify the most appropriate result, they're useful in helping identify *how to present results*. The persistence of dates within queries suggests that the searcher is trying to either narrow or sort her search results. The fix, as the *Financial Times* found, is to enable searchers to sort *and* filter by date, as you can see from the search results page shown in Figure 8.13.

FIGURE 8.13

The *Financial Times* allows searchers to sort *and* filter search results by date.

Financial Times could take this approach just a little further by setting the sorting to default to "Date" when date information is included in the query. (The current default for all queries seems to be "Relevance.")

Finding URLs in query logs isn't so strange; searcher sees boxes on a page, searcher fills it in with a URL. Why should a search entry box be any different than an address entry box? In fact, because it happened so often, IBM Software found it worth addressing. Rather than punish searchers with an unpleasant 404-like "no results found" experience, IBM simply taught its search engine to redirect searchers to the desired page, as specified by the URL entered. It was a simple and straightforward way to show its searchers respect.

Designing Search Results Around Specialized Content Types

You can also tune your search results when you know that you have specific types of content that searchers might find especially interesting. In Chapter 3, "Pattern Analysis," we used our Michigan State University example to illustrate how you might uncover potential content types that occur again and again in your site. Once you have those types in place, they serve as wonderful "building blocks" for tuning your search results in a powerful way.

In the example shown in Figure 8.14, the searcher is looking for a product that includes the number 1012. Hewlett Packard's search engine has been taught to guess that such numeric strings are quite likely to be products. And HP has already identified a variety of content types—"Product overview," "Supplies, options & accessories," and so on—which are associated with products. (These are displayed in the center of the page under "Product quick links.") In effect, HP has determined that queries for products ought to have certain content types shown automatically and expects that these are valuable to searchers. In fact, they seem far more valuable than the rough results found by the search engine (to the right, under "Search results").

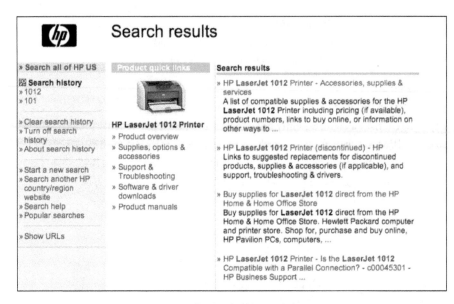

FIGURE 8.14

When Hewlett Packard's search engine senses a product search, it automatically displays product-related content types (for example, "Software & driver downloads") in the center of the page, while raw search results are displayed to the right.

Hewlett Packard's approach is very intelligent—in fact, it's a souped-up version of best bets. HP has already done the hard work of determining what its content types are, and likely tags them as such in its content management system. It takes advantage of that effort by exposing appropriate content types when it encounters a specialized search, in this case, a product query.

Interestingly, HP shows content types that are geared toward existing customers rather than ones who might be considering purchasing this particular product. The company's research may have shown that it has more existing customers search its site for product information than prospects. And we've all heard how it's cheaper to keep a customer than to acquire one.

Using SSA to Help Determine Search Scoping

Martin Belam, Information Architect, Guardian News & Media—www.currybet.net

One way to help searchers to get to the best result quicker is by "scoping" their search: limiting their results to content similar to the page they are currently viewing. For example, if they use the search box on a page in your "press office" section of the Web site, you would only return results from pages published by the press office, not the site as a whole.

While this can be very helpful to some searchers, particularly on sites with large silos of unrelated content, it can also second-guess their intentions. If you scope your content incorrectly, you might have made it nearly impossible for the searchers to locate the information they need.

Site search analytics can help you to understand whether "scoped" search is really helping your searchers, but you have to make sure you are measuring the right things. If you have three different scoped search boxes on your site (for example, the news section, help section, and documentation section of your site or intranet), it is important that you can slice your data to examine behavior in each of those scopes in isolation. You'll want to be able to see the top search terms that have been used on a particular area of the site, and you'll also be very interested in those searches that have generated no results.

On the guardian.co.uk Web site, we scope search based on the section of the site that the searcher is currently visiting. This can get quite granular, so that if you are on guardian.co.uk/culture, you only receive results from our culture coverage. If you drill down further within that to the music section, then search results are restricted to just returning content that has been tagged with music. Search log analysis allows us to check whether this is helpful or not. For example, in January 2010, one of the top 10 searches on the music section of the site was for wire (see Figure 8.15). Because of scoping, we can guarantee that the searcher is only going to get articles about the recently reformed '70s post-punk band, rather than our extensive coverage of the critically acclaimed TV show *The Wire*.

continues on next page

Using SSA to Help Determine Search Scoping (continued)

Correlation Summary	
Total	
Internal Search Results - Filters = Music	
Internal Search Terms	
1.	mick karn
2.	british sea power
3.	brother
4.	anna calvi
5.	kanye west
6.	mozart pop
7.	james blake
8.	adele
9.	gerry rafferty
10.	wire

FIGURE 8.15
The top 10 searches within the Music scope of guardian.co.uk in the first weeks of January 2010.

Looking further down the most popular searches, however, reveals that we have a problem. In the top 40 searches on the Guardian's music area at guardian.co.uk/music, we also see frequent queries for top columnist Charlie Brooker and for the crossword. These are most certainly not music-specific queries. Our answer is to make sure that more general, site-wide editorial best bets are also retrieved within a scoped search's results. This gives the searchers the best of both worlds. If their query is specific to the area of the site, they get the narrow focus of scoped search. If their query is a navigational one, aimed at jumping context to another area of the site, then best bets will take them there (see Figure 8.16).

This means you'll have to regularly monitor the generic queries within a scope to make sure that you are picking up all of the popular searches that would benefit from being an editorial best bet.

Using SSA to Help Determine Search Scoping (continued)

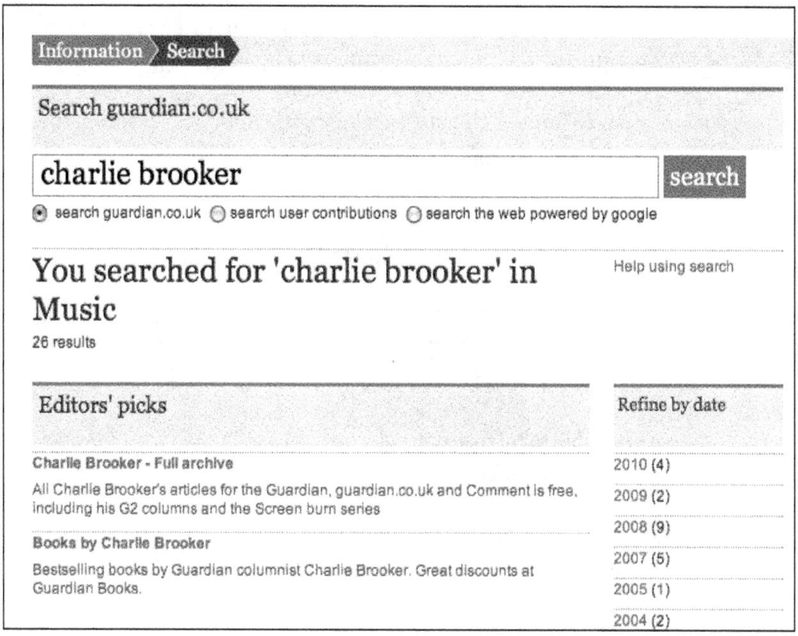
Information
Search
Search guardian.co.uk
charlie brooker
search
search guardian.co.uk
search user contributions
search the web powered by google
You searched for 'charlie brooker' in Music
26 results
Help using search
Editors' picks
Charlie Brooker - Full archive
All Charlie Brooker's articles for the Guardian, guardian.co.uk and Comment is free, including his G2 columns and the Screen burn series
Books by Charlie Brooker
Bestselling books by Guardian columnist Charlie Brooker. Great discounts at Guardian Books.
Refine by date
2010 (4)
2009 (2)
2008 (9)
2007 (5)
2005 (1)
2004 (2)

FIGURE 8.16
This search originated in the Music area of guardian.co.uk, as indicated by "You searched for 'charlie brooker' in Music." Although the 26 results returned are specific to that area of the site, the "Editor's picks," our label for best bets, are generic and direct the searcher to useful links outside of the music scope.

Summary

- Identify gaps in your search engine's index by finding top queries with zero results and then identifying which aren't retrieving results because there *is no content* to match searchers' needs.

- Make your search entry box the right width by measuring the width of your queries.

- Analyze queries to identify odd or unexpected queries and query syntax that your search engine should be configured to support.

- SSA can identify good candidates for best bets and, when you have multiple best bets for a particular query, help you prioritize their order.

- Use SSA to help create a cleaned-up version of terms for query auto-completion.

- SSA can improve your null results page by providing a list of your site's most popular search terms to choose from or similar search terms based on synonyms.

- Use SSA to better support query refinement (instead of relying on Advanced Search interfaces).

- When multi-field search interfaces make more sense than a single box, use SSA to help determine which fields or facets to make searchable.

- Look for specialized (and very important) query types and then develop specialized search results for those queries.

- Conversely, identify important, consistently appearing content types, and use them to power results for important query types (like product names).

- Use SSA to help determine and tune search "scopes" or zones within your site's content.

CHAPTER 9

Practical Tips for Improving Site Navigation and Metadata

Improving Contextual Navigation for
  Specific Content Types   144
Creating a Better Site Index   148
Testing and Tuning Metadata Values Important   150
Summary   154

J ust as site search analytics can improve your site's search system, it can also increase findability in other ways. In this chapter, we'll show you a few approaches to improve your site's navigation and metadata based on analyzing your query data.

Improving Contextual Navigation for Specific Content Types

You've got 'em: important page types that occur again and again, deep within your site. Perhaps they are pages that describe the benefits that your products bring. Or they are bios of each of the high-priced consultants you hire out. Or they are your intranet's critical policies—the ones that all employees had better follow.

Whatever these pages are, they behave consistently—in fact, they may be built by your CMS using the same template. And they are often critical to your organization's success, because if these pages don't work well, you may be in deep trouble.

They also may generate quite a bit of search traffic. For example, User Interface Engineering found that over 50% of search traffic on a major commerce site was generated from the department, gallery, and product pages deep inside the site, noting that "most users clicked on more than three links before they decided to search," as shown in Figure 9.1.[1]

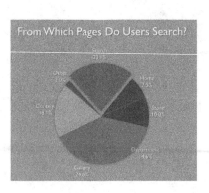

FIGURE 9.1
Search activity can and often will happen on pages other than your site's main page, as this example from UIE shows (www.uie.com/articles/time_search).

---

[1] From "Spending Quality Time with Your Search Log," UIE Web site; Jared Spool; January 6, 2010; http://www.uie.com/articles/time_search/

These deep page types clearly deserve your attention, and you can use SSA in a few ways to improve them:

- **Identify frequently occurring (and valuable) page types.** In Chapter 3, "Pattern Analysis," I showed you a method for using your queries to identify page types that searchers seem to be requesting. Once you know what page types are common to your site, you can move on to these next tasks.

- **Determine what's missing from each page type.** Assuming your analytics application will allow you to do so, analyze the frequent queries generated by each page type by starting with a few samples of each type. Look over each sample's queries. Do you see any patterns? You might find that users are looking to move to another, related kind of content; these *desire paths* might suggest adding contextual navigation links to the page type (see Figure 9.2).[2] I looked at three samples of AIGA's event pages in Figures 9.3, 9.5, and 9.7. You'll see the results in Figure 9.4, 9.6, and 9.8. Or you might notice that users are requesting that more information be included in the page type (which means you've now identified a way to improve the content in that page type).

FIGURE 9.2
A desire path worn by those navigating this lawn. Are there similar paths that have been created by people trying to navigate your site?

---

2   Desire paths are desired forms of navigation that a system currently doesn't support. You'll often see them in a park or on a college quadrangle: paths worn into the dirt by constant use, unanticipated by the space's planners. More on desire paths in Wikipedia: http://en.wikipedia.org/wiki/Desire_path

EVENTS

NITTY GRITTY: Value Pricing = Greater Income + Happier Clients

Wednesday, December 10, 2008 — December 10, 2008   Houston
9:30 CT

Learning to use value pricing is learning to quit selling your time (a very finite resource!) and start selling your knowledge, something with infinite room to grow. Value pricing is the idea that a fair price relates more to the client's expectations and alternatives, and bottom line return on a design project than it does to the time taken to create the design. Understanding and using value pricing means you will earn more money for the time you spend working; yet adopting a value pricing mind set is difficult for many design professionals. Join Pam Bryan at the Nitty-Gritty and learn:

- Why your prospect's reference points matter and how you can change them
- What determines your prospect's perception of value

Query	Frequency
brand standard pricing	1
design pricing	1
design quote	1
how much should we charge	1
how to price	1
letterhead pricing	1
price guide	1
pricing	1
pricing + rate	1
pricing chart	1
pricing jobs	1
pricing work	1
rates	1
salary	1
student pricing	1
what to ask before taking on project	1
what to charge clients	1
work prices	1

FIGURE 9.3
An AIGA.org event on value pricing (www.aiga.org/content.cfm/event-detail?eid=21627029)...

FIGURE 9.4
...is the starting point for these queries—many of which are about pricing.

EVENTS

The Business of Design - Professional Relationships & Pricing

Wednesday, April 30, 2008   Baltimore
5 p.m.

University of Baltimore
Student Center, Multipurpose Room (5th Floor)
21 W. Mt. Royal Ave., Baltimore MD

Join AIGA and University of Baltimore for three informative panel discussions focused on the Business of Design. Topics covered will include: marketing, branding, taxes, financial concerns, building professional relationships, and pricing your work. Moderated by Ed Gold, Author & Professor at the University of Baltimore.

Third Night: Wednesday April 30th

Query	Frequency
pricing	5
What to charge for publications design	1
creative business	1
freelance	1
graphic design pricing	1
how to price	1
logo design	1
packaging pricing	1
price	1
pricing guide	1
pricing projects	1
salarium minimun	1

FIGURE 9.5
Another AIGA.org event (www.aiga.org/content.cfm/event-detail?eid=17487113) also addresses pricing...

FIGURE 9.6
...and is also the starting point for many queries regarding the subject of pricing.

EVENTS

AIGA Annual Student Portfolio Review

Saturday, May 5, 2007   Boston
9:30am - 3:30pm

Trustees Room, Massachusetts College of Art
Tower Building, 11th Floor,
621 Huntington Avenue, Boston, MA 02115

SOLD OUT! Waiting list spots only. The AIGA Student Portfolio Event is a day-long event designed to give you—a graduating senior or graduate-level student about to embark on a career in the design industry—advice, insight, and useful information about how to present yourself and your work. Here is your chance to have a professional look at your portfolio in a no-risk, non-competitive environment. You can practice your interview skills and get honest feedback about your portfolio and resume. Why you should attend... You will receive thoughtful, constructive, one-on-one evaluation of your work by an array of design professionals—art directors, media producers, educators, and hiring

Query	Frequency
portfolio review	3
Utah portfolio review	1
aiga portfolio bootcamp	1
aiga student portfolio review raliegh, nc	1
boston portfolio	1
bowling green ohio	1
dallas	1
mentoring	1
new orleans	1
portfolio review new orleans	1
portfolio review pittsburgh	1
student portfolio	1
student portfolios	1

FIGURE 9.7

This AIGA.org event (www.aiga.org/content.cfm/event-detail?eid=12771382) is about student portfolios...

FIGURE 9.8

...and, not surprisingly, it leads to many queries about portfolios.

- **Identify problematic members of a particular page type.** While you're comparing your page type samples, you might find one that's an outlier. For example, one of your 15 product description pages (or, in the case of AIGA, one of your event pages) may generate very different types of queries or a much higher volume of queries. Is that particular page broken in some particular way? Is it poorly labeled, titled, or written? Is it missing some critical contextual navigation? Or, conversely, is there something special about that particular product that suggests you reconsider how navigation works for your other product descriptions? Now you have an interesting question to consider, and you can explore it further using a qualitative user research technique.

Each of the event pages I sampled indicated that users were interested in getting more information on each of the page's respective topics. There are many potential reasons for this; for example, the users weren't able to make the event in person but were interested in the topic. Or they visited the page after the event had taken place and wanted to know about the topic. Or they got to the page from a Google search, and it wasn't quite what they needed, so they used the AIGA site search to see if it had what they were looking for.

Whatever the case may be, since these events seem to serve as good landing pages for their topics, AIGA may want to invest in linking to relevant (and more static) content on its site from within each event page.

Creating a Better Site Index

A–Z site indices are like the sad, neglected vacant lots you find in many cities—full of trash and weeds, yet so prominent throughout the site. They're often just a single link from anywhere in the site and therefore so full of potential. This prime real estate is usually wasted because developing and maintaining an alphabetical index for a large Web site require much more work than most people anticipate. And when your site is really a collection of separate, distributed subsites, many of which are off the grid, the problem gets even worse. After all, you can't index what you don't know about.

You might decide that a site index simply isn't worth the bother. After all, indices work best for users who know what they're looking for, but in those cases, search systems are almost always a better option.

If you *do* decide to maintain an index—because your users already rely upon it, or because your search system is in "transition" at the moment—you can build an alphabetical index around your common search queries. In effect, your index will be designed around your searchers' most pressing information needs. This works especially well if you are already building an extensive set of best bet search results around those common queries. Michigan State University has done just that.

MSU has an initiative in place for creating best bets for hundreds of its most frequent queries. As you might expect, it stores these results in a database. It didn't take long for the smart folks there to realize that their database could output those results as a single alphabetized list just as easily as it could match individual results to a specific search query (see Figure 9.9).

FIGURE 9.9
Each entry in MSU.edu's A–Z index is a common query ("keyword") and is linked to its best bet search result (under "Description").

The result is compelling. Not only has MSU reused its editorial effort in an innovative way, but, in effect, it has also cracked the nut of Web site alphabetical indices. It has addressed maintenance challenges by basing its index on an ongoing stream of popular queries, leveraging existing best bet maintenance efforts. Additionally, the index cuts across the many content "silos"—departments and divisions—found in huge organizations like a university. Rather than trying to represent each silo in the index evenly— a fool's errand—MSU defers to searchers' queries as the arbiter of what will and won't be included in the index. As a result, MSU provides its users with a living, breathing A–Z index that spans many silos and requires almost no additional expense beyond its existing best bet initiative.

Testing and Tuning Metadata Values Important

Every domain is changing. And every domain's vocabulary of descriptive metadata should, naturally, change as well, but all too typically it lags behind. This is especially true in dynamic, rapidly changing domains, especially those related to technology or the hard sciences. It's simply difficult and expensive to keep up. Fortunately, SSA offers a variety of approaches to help you evaluate and maintain metadata values, which fall into three categories:

- Testing terms using the "query test."

- Deriving terms through "reverse lookup."

- Tracking appearances, disappearances, and trends among terms.

Putting Metadata Through the "Query Test"

You can test your metadata by treating them as queries and, well, trying them out. Do they retrieve relevant documents? And how do they compare with equivalent queries? After all, metadata should be close to the language of searchers; queries *already are.*

That's not entirely fair. Metadata are *not* queries, and the people responsible for metadata have to balance the nature of the content and its language with users' natural language. But you still may find this test instructive:

1. Choose a manageable number of your most frequent queries. Say, 25.

2. See if those queries have synonymous metadata values. For example, campus map may be a common query; its closest metadata equivalent might be "map."

3. Are there any queries that don't have similar metadata terms? Great, you've just identified potential gaps in your metadata vocabulary that need to be filled.

4. Measure your frequent queries' relevance and precision. (This is what Vanguard did in Chapter 1, "How Site Search Analytics Can Save Your Butt.")

5. Do the same for the corresponding metadata. In other words, try them as queries using the same metrics.

6. Now see how well they compare. If your metadata don't perform as well as their synonymous frequent queries, they might merit another look and possibly replacement. For example, if your metadata term is "water closet," but the query toilet is much more effective, you might want to replace the former with the latter.

Using "Reverse Lookup" to Identify New and Problematic Terms

Just as you can test metadata values as queries and see what documents they retrieve, you might consider doing the opposite: start with the documents and try to determine which metadata values ought to be matched with them. To do this, you'll need an analytics tool that can track the queries that found a particular document:

- **Start with a small set (say 20) of important documents.** "Important" can mean different things, such as popular (in terms of showing up in search results or being clicked through from those results), authoritative, or subjectively important, according to the needs of your business and its customers.

- **List the queries that retrieve those important documents.** You'll either need an analytics application that can handle both clickstream analysis and SSA, or the willingness to do a lot of parsing and crunching by hand.

- **Determine if there are metadata that correspond with those queries.** (This is similar to our "query test"—we're matching metadata terms and queries.) So, for example, you may find that the query no-iron shirts comes up a lot on your clothing site, but there are no corresponding metadata terms. If that's the case, then you've identified a gap in your metadata. Consider creating a new term, or if you can, recasting an existing term in more contemporary, user-friendly language.

- **Use extra credit.** If possible, **try this same exercise only with new documents.** This will be especially helpful as you try to maintain the currency of your metadata values in the face of your domain's new content.

Tracking Metadata Trends

Identifying new queries that are trending upward is a great way to keep the scope of your metadata updated. You may be able to identify terms in a particular batch of queries that were never searched for on your site before and use those terms to develop new metadata values.

Any brand new query—whether searched a thousand times or just once—will register as having infinite growth, as its starting point was 0. Because brand new queries grow at the same rate, regardless of their search volume, you'll want to focus on the more frequently searched new queries. So, if your clothing site has two new queries—hoodie, with 71 searches, and crocs, with 449—you'll clearly want to focus your energy on crocs.

In the case of existing queries that are trending up, it can be a bit tricky to determine which ones truly merit your attention (see Table 9.1). Some queries might start small and spike up quickly, while others may already be frequent but are growing at substantial rates. Which are more important?

TABLE 9.1

COMPARING TWO TRENDING QUERIES				
Query	Last Month	Current Month	# Growth	% Growth
2010 marketing strategy	2 queries	91 queries	89 queries	4,450%
Travel guidelines	594 queries	805 queries	211 queries	36%

Spikes in query activity. Which is more noteworthy?

The more common query certainly deserves attention. It may have a much slower growth rate, but its overall growth (in terms of actual queries) is more than twice as high. And it's already an important query. If there's no corresponding metadata value, you might scratch your head and ask yourself why not. If corresponding metadata are already in place, then you don't have much to do, although something else—unrelated to metadata— might be happening. Seasonal spike perhaps?

The less common query—2010 marketing strategy—is interesting in a different way. It's spiked much more quickly, but is it real or an anomaly? Put it on your watchlist, and give it more time to "prove itself" worthy of joining your stodgy, oak-paneled metadata club. Adding a new term to a vocabulary has long-term implications, and it shouldn't be done in any manner that hints at flightiness or impulsiveness. So keep your eye on spikes that emanate from the middle torso and determine whether you've got a flash in the pan or something of long-term importance. If it's the former, you might be better off addressing the information need that it represents with a lighter scale touch, such as implementing a best bet search result to ensure that when it is searched, it retrieves something of value.

Just as a query might suddenly spike, the reverse is true as well: queries can begin to drop out of sight, albeit a bit more gradually than they rise. You'll want to determine if a more up-to-date variant is available to replace a moribund term.

Keep in mind that eliminating metadata values is a very dicey proposition. You may already have a lot invested in a particular term, in the sense that it's been used to tag a significant amount of your content. Retracting a term will have an impact on each of those documents. Now missing an old term, will their chance of being found greatly diminish? You'll want to consider replacing stale metadata values with more viable synonyms. Hopefully, you'll have a content management system or some other automated means in place to make such changes globally; otherwise, you'll have a lot of tedious manual labor to struggle with.

Summary

- Identify specific content types that generate a lot of search traffic and use this information to improve your site's contextual navigation.

- Build a better alphabetical index for your site by basing index entries on your frequent query terms.

- Tune and test your metadata by comparing it with the tone, coverage, and trends of your searchers' common queries.

CHAPTER 10

Practical Tips for Improving Content

Determining Which Content You Should Get Rid of   156
Plugging Content Gaps   156
Making Relevant Content Even More Relevant   158
Expanding Your Understanding of Users'
    Content Interests   159
Getting Marketing to Do the Right Thing   161
Getting Content Owners to Do the Right Thing   162
Summary   164

S ite search analytics doesn't just help you improve your site's *findability*. In this chapter, we'll cover a few ways it can lead directly to better content.

Determining Which Content You Should Get Rid of

These days, many organizations are falling over themselves to hire content strategists to help them figure out what content to get rid of, and for good reason: ROT (Redundant, Outdated, and Trivial) content misinforms and confuses. It's expensive to maintain and even more expensive *not* to maintain. It damages the search experience as well, because no matter how brilliantly you've designed your site's search system, poor content will invariably clutter your search results.

There are many ways that organizations identify ROT. It might be content that's never or rarely been accessed, according to server logs. (Unverified rumor: 90% of Microsoft.com's content has *never* been accessed—not once!) It might be content that is too old or has no clear owner. SSA can provide another criterion to consider. For example, perhaps content that is *not* retrieved by short head queries (say, your 100 most common queries) should be considered as potential ROT. After all, if important queries don't find it, there's a chance it's not especially relevant.

Sandia National Labs took a slightly different SSA-based approach. It compared content that's been spidered—in other words, that the search engine knows about—but was rarely if ever accessed. If the search engine knows about it, but searchers don't find it, perhaps it should be weeded?

Plugging Content Gaps

Conversely, does your site or intranet have the content it ought to? Using SSA to answer this question is both deceptively simple and highly effective.

Review your most frequent zero result queries on a regular basis: weekly for most sites, and daily for commerce sites whose customers and products are highly dynamic. Try variants of each query to validate that the documents are simply not there. If they're not, the solution is relatively simple: create new content.

Of course, getting new content created can be tricky. It's not always clear that you *should* support queries that are retrieving zero results. If your alternative medicine drugstore site keeps getting queries for Nyquil, you probably don't want to start selling Vicks products.

But there is an opportunity there. Instead of simply showing a zero results page, why not provide an explanation of *why* you don't sell Nyquil? Or why you strongly recommend alternative medical products over commercial pharmaceuticals in general? Instead of punishing the users, you have a great opportunity to provide them with some useful information.

And while we're on the subject of punishment, you can beat up on the person in your organization who is shirking his responsibility for creating content. For example, at Michigan State University, freedom of information was a frequent query that wasn't retrieving any content. Ironically, the university's Freedom of Information Officer hadn't made herself particularly easy to find. So MSU hit on an ingenious temporary solution: make her staff directory a best bet search result that would be retrieved by the query freedom of information (see Figure 10.1). That way the officer's contact information was made to serve as a placeholder search result until she created a more helpful page about freedom of information at MSU (see Figure 10.2).

Search MSU

Search MSU   Find People   Browse A-Z

| freedom of information | | Search |

MSU Keywords found these best bets for "freedom of information":

Freedom of Information Act Officer *Official Site*
isweb1.cl.msu.edu/msusearch/msupeople.php?lname=armentrout&fname=ellen

FIGURE 10.1
Now when you search MSU's site for "freedom of information," you get a best bet result...

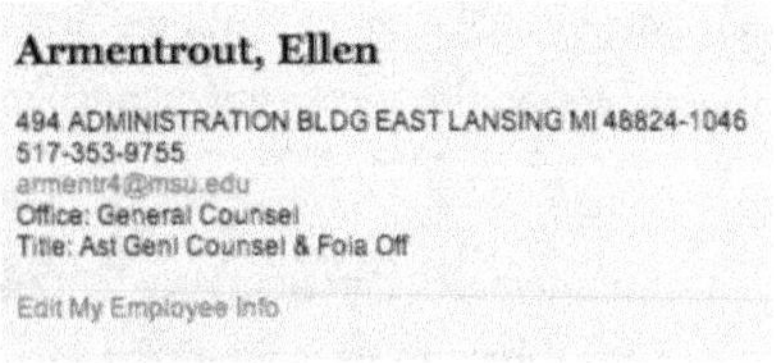

FIGURE 10.2
...the FOIA officer's
directory entry!

Making Relevant Content Even More Relevant

Your analysis of null results reports may uncover a different problem: you have the relevant documents, but for some reason they're not being retrieved (or, if they are, they're hopelessly too far down the results list to be noticed). When relevant documents aren't matching searchers' queries, the culprits are usually one or more of these:

- **Deficient titling:** This is a common problem in large organizations where many different authors handle titling documents. When it comes to their own documents, authors can be a bit narcissistic. They don't always realize or remember that their document will be accessed as part of a much larger collection of documents. So their document on expense reporting guidelines gets lost in the search results pages because it's been titled too broadly ("Travel"), narrowly ("Taxi Receipts"), too jargony ("Using the ReimburseX System V8.2"), or too obscurely ("Policy #29-b.37").

- **Deficient or poorly applied metadata:** If your search system takes advantage of the metadata associated with your document (say, to support fielded searching), searchers will experience problems akin to poor titling. (And unfortunately, poor titling and poor metadata often go together.)

- **Poor writing:** Is there something missing from relevant documents that simply ought to be there? Intuit's Christine Connors found this to be the case. Users were frequently searching for the phrase get back overpaid wages and striking out. These terms ought to have been included in the appropriate Intuit page. They weren't, and the fix was obvious and easy to implement. Now it might not sound fair to call such a document "deficient"—the writing itself was fine—but it was missing something that should have been there all along.

These issues are all diagnosable and all fixable, but they may require some social reengineering. We'll cover that in the last two hacks in this chapter.

Expanding Your Understanding of Users' Content Interests

When searchers ask your site—through a query—for information about a particular topic, the *way* they ask it reveals much about their understanding of that topic (and, often, some surprises). One way to do this is by exploring the other terms that searchers use in combination with the particular term that you're interested in analyzing to see what sort of *adjacent* interests (and corresponding content) can be deduced. This is especially useful with queries for newer terms where you don't have much understanding of what else the searchers might be interested in beyond the term itself.

For example, the BBC encountered a spike in queries for a company called *Farepak*, and used a couple different approaches to learn more about it. The report in Figure 10.3 shows one week's worth of BBC.co.uk queries that include the term Farepak.

Keyword Analysis (BBC tab scope) for : farepak

- 'Search Term' shows search terms containing the chosen keyword
- 'Total' is the number of searches for the search term
- 'Chart %' is percentage of the queries shown in this table (not of all seaches containing the search term)

Use right-hand-click to export the table to MS Excel

No.	Search Term	Total	Chart	Chart %
1	farepak	3,405		87.6 %
2	farepak hampers	323		8.3 %
3	farepak hamper	15		0.4 %
4	news on farepak hampers	10		0.3 %
5	www.farepak.co.uk	9		0.2 %
6	farepak food	9		0.2 %
7	farepak news	9		0.2 %
8	farepak vouchers	7		0.2 %
9	working lunch farepak hampers	6		0.2 %
10	farepak food & gifts	6		0.2 %
11	farepak in administration	4		0.1 %
12	farepak*	4		0.1 %
13	farepak foods	4		0.1 %
14	farepak voucher company	4		0.1 %
15	watch dog farepak	4		0.1 %
16	northwest farepak	3		0.1 %
17	farepak bust	3		0.1 %
18	farepak in scotland	3		0.1 %
19	farepak hamp	3		0.1 %
20	farepak bdo	3		0.1 %
21	farepak christmas vouchers	3		0.1 %

FIGURE 10.3
Queries at BBC.co.uk that include the term Farepak.

You'll immediately notice that many of the queries include the term hamper. That's because Farepak was, essentially, a club that negotiated special deals for customers for the holiday season: Christmas hampers are baskets of food that customers had paid for in advance. Farepak was running into financial difficulties—ultimately reported by the BBC (see http://news.bbc.co.uk/2/hi/business/6124406.stm)—and clearly many were interested in the story's developments. Farepak's troubles can also be sussed out from other queries shown here, like Farepak in administration ("in administration" means the same thing as "bankrupt" does in the U.S.), and Farepak bust. Now the Farepak story starts to become clearer, and the BBC could adjust its coverage—and its content—accordingly.

Analyzing other terms that were searched within the same session as Farepak also gleans some useful benefits, as the next report in Figure 10.4 demonstrates. This Amazon-like "people who searched for... also searched for..." approach provides a clearer understanding of common misspellings (helpful if you're building a thesaurus or some other capacity for handling equivalent terms). More importantly, it provides useful semantic clues, like connecting Farepak to Watchdog, a BBC consumer affairs program that may have reported on the story.

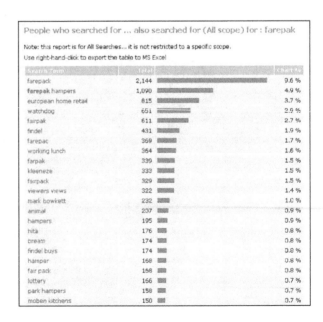

FIGURE 10.4
BBC.co.uk queries
that occurred within
the same session as
Farepak.

Are there topics that show up in your search logs that merit further exploration? You might learn more about them and their context by seeing what else users searched them with. Then develop your content in response to what you've learned.

Getting Marketing to Do the Right Thing

Jargon, specifically in branding products and services, has been a bone of contention between marketers and UX people, like, forever. (And you already know whose side I'll be taking in this argument.)

Clearly, there are some cases when a brand name makes or breaks a product's success. But just some: not every brand name can compare with, say, Coca-Cola, because not every product is backed by a similar budget or has the decades of exposure that are required to establish it within a market. In most cases, avoiding jargon in favor of plain language that actually means something to your customers will yield better results. SSA can help your organization decide on whether to use jargon or plain language terminology (and, of course, help you determine just what that plain language ought to be).

Washtenaw Community College (www.wccnet.edu) faced exactly this challenge. Like many academic institutions, WCC offers a variety of Web-based educational programs. They sported some interesting brand names, like "College on Demand" (aka "COD") and "FlexEd." But students weren't signing up at nearly the rates that were expected.

WCC's marketing staff were considering some traditional advertising remedies: mass mailings of brochures, creation of posters, and other measures that would introduce these terms to target audiences. Such an approach can't guarantee success, but considering its reliance on broadcasting to a large audience, it's guaranteed to be expensive. WCC's Web team, armed with its secret SSA weapon, had another idea: compare the frequency of queries for brand names with their plain language equivalents.

The numbers were eye opening. During the time period studied, COD ranked as the 101st most popular query, College on Demand clocked in at #259, and FlexEd at #389. Compare those rankings with the best plain language equivalent, online, at position #22. Additionally, online was included as part of 213 other queries (see Figure 10.5).

FIGURE 10.5
WCC query ranks:
online is far more
popular than the other,
more jargony terms.

query rank	query
#22	online*
#101	COD
#259	College on Demand
#389	FlexTrack

The result? WCC relabeled much of its content with plain language terms, ensuring that its content already spoke the language of its customers, rather than investing heavily in training customers to use WCC's language. The brand names didn't necessarily go away, but they weren't relied upon to match content with users' needs.

Getting Content Owners to Do the Right Thing

Chances are if your organization has more than one content author, it has a thick set of policies and procedures to guide their work. And chances are that your content authors will ignore them. Not because they're bad people, but because the activity of creating content is necessarily a very focused one. You're typically thinking deeply about what you're writing or editing, not of the bigger picture of how your content will fit into the broader collection of documents that populates a Web site or intranet. When you combine myopic content creation with a disregard for following conventions for style, titling, and tagging documents, you're left with documents that won't get found.

Sandia National Labs dealt with this problem in a very innovative way. For its 50 most frequent queries, Web staff regularly record which documents show up at position #1 on the search results page. If and when that top document falls out of position #1, the staff alert the document's owner and begin a healthy dialogue about why this has happened.

Given that the drop often has something to do with not following policies and procedures, the content owner is more likely to understand their value—and the natural urge to compete (and win) helps content owners see that their content is indeed part of something bigger. A secondary benefit is the creation of the dialogue itself—in large organizations, Web staff and content authors often have little opportunity or clear incentives to talk.

Summary

- Identify the content that's not being found by common queries—maybe it's time to weed it out or at least make it less prominent.

- Use SSA to identify content gaps; consider these gaps as opportunities to grow your offerings.

- Diagnose content problems with SSA, such as deficient titling, poorly applied metadata, or poor writing.

- See what types of queries co-occur with specific queries you want to study; you'll get a sense of what content should co-occur.

- Squash ill-considered reliance on jargon and brand names by finding better plain-language alternatives among your query data.

- Get content owners to finally follow content guidelines by using query data to show them how terribly their content fails when they ignore the guidelines.

CHAPTER 11

Bridging Web Analytics and User Experience

Data and Design: Never the Twain Shall Meet   166
The Case for Integrated Problem Solving   168
Creating a Single User Research Brain Within
   Your Organization   177
Site Search Analytics: The Natural Boundary Object   182

I hope that this book has, by now, convinced you that site search analytics is indeed a valuable user research technique. Still, there are many people out there in both the user experience and web analytics communities who don't take advantage of SSA. Even stranger, practitioners from both communities should be analyzing queries *together*. After all, SSA has something to offer to both: analytics folks generally want to derive insights from whatever huge store of behavioral data they can get their hands on. Meanwhile, the data's semantic richness helps establish users' intent as do many of the core research methods that UX practitioners rely upon. So why aren't they sitting down to analyze query data together?

Well, the truth is, they're not doing much of anything together. To grossly overgeneralize, it's very much a right brain/left brain situation—they are two very different types of people who intuitively try to solve problems in very different ways. And because they live in separate organizational silos, web analytics and user experience folks simply don't mix that much to begin with.

But as different as they may be, their respective problem-solving approaches are incredibly complementary. In fact, they're really two halves of the same brain. So wouldn't it be great to get them to think—and work—together?

In this chapter, we'll step back from site search analytics to look at these communities' respective and complementary skills, and argue for their greater integration. Then we'll return one last time to SSA to offer it as a *boundary object*—a common method around which both fields can coalesce and eventually collaborate.

Data and Design: Never the Twain Shall Meet

Here's an interesting headline in Figure 11.1 involving a really well-known designer and a really, really well-known Web search company.

And here's another headline in Figure 11.2 involving the same two parties, not three years later.

FIGURE 11.1

"Google just got Doug Bowman. Smart move by Google. This is their best acquisition to date." (37 Signals, May 2006)[1]

FIGURE 11.2

"Google's Data Fetish Drives Away Its Top Designer." (ValleyWag, March 2009)[2]

---

1   May 26, 2006; Signals vs. Noise (37 Signals' blog) http://37signals.com/svn/archives2/googles_best_acquisition_to_date_doug_bowman.php

2   March 20, 2009; ValleyWag http://valleywag.gawker.com/5177144/googles-data-fetish-drives-away-its-top-designer

Doug Bowman's journey in and out of the GooglePlex is a very telling one. Smart designer gets snapped up by smart, engineering-driven company, to great applause. Company assigns him a newly minted senior role—Visual Design Lead—and charges him with helping "establish a common visual language across all [its] collaborative and communication products."[3] Designer finds that it's not exactly easy to inject design thinking into a well-established engineering culture. And, after a couple years, finally flees after being asked to use data to justify his design decisions once too often. ("Ummm, Doug? We'll need some data to determine whether that line should be three, four, or five pixels wide."[4])

While it may sound silly to test the performance of a line's width (we're not making this up) or the relative merits of 41 shades of blue,[5] you really can't argue with Google's success. Then again, if you'd been following his career, you really can't argue with Doug Bowman's success. Who's right here: the UX guy or the data-driven engineers? More importantly, whose approach to solving problems is the better one?

The Case for Integrated Problem Solving

Before we select a winner, let's take a closer look at both approaches. Table 11.1 attempts—in, admittedly, highly generalized terms—to show the differences between the practices of web analytics and user experience.

The two practices really are quite different and, as Doug Bowman found, don't necessarily jive very well—especially in organizations, like Google, that are so strongly skewed in one direction. Yet they each have something to offer and are often attempting to address the very same kinds of design problems. Given that they both succeed, to varying degrees, there must be merit in both. And if each has merit without the other, on its own, each must be incomplete.

---

3   May 27, 2006: StopDesign (Doug Bowman's site) http://stopdesign.com/archive/2006/05/27/going-to-google.html

4   March 20, 2009: StopDesign http://stopdesign.com/archive/2009/03/20/goodbye-google.html

5   March 3, 2009: *New York Times* www.nytimes.com/2009/03/01/business/01marissa.html

TABLE 11.1

COMPARING WEB ANALYTICS AND USER EXPERIENCE		
	Web Analytics	User Experience
What they analyze	Users' behaviors (*what's* happening)	Users' intentions and motives (*why* those things happen)
What methods they commonly employ	*Quantitative* methods to determine what's happening	*Qualitative* methods for explaining why things happen
What they're trying to achieve	Helps the *organization* meet its known goals (expressed as KPI)	Helps *users* achieve their goals (often expressed as primary tasks or topics of interest)
How they use data	To measure performance through *benchmarking* and *monitoring* (top-down analysis)	"Plays" with data to uncover *patterns* and *surprises* (bottom-up analysis)
What kinds of data they use	*Statistical data* ("real" data in large volumes and full of errors)	*Conceptual data* (descriptive data in small volumes, artificially generated in lab environment, and full of errors)
Where the practitioners come from	Backgrounds in *engineering or math*	Backgrounds in *social sciences, humanities, or the arts*

For example, if you're analyzing clickstream data, you're trying to figure out *what* happens as users move through your site. But you won't get too far solely relying upon that method to answer *why* they do what they do. Or, if you're running a field study, you might get a great sense of *why* people behave as they do, but your picture of *what* is going on is hugely limited and limiting.

But here's the good news: as much as each practice is incomplete, they're chock-full of incredibly complementary dichotomies. When these two incomplete problem-solving approaches are integrated, we can achieve a far more balanced understanding of both *what* is happening with our sites and *why*. After all, *it's not much use to know what is happening if you don't know why*. Conversely, *it's not much use to understand why things are happening when you don't understand what they were in the first place*. When you integrate the what and the why, you'll be creating something of a powerful new decision-making engine for your organization—and all sorts of new opportunities for your organization to leap ahead of its competition.

Let's look at just a few examples of how web analytics and user experience approaches can complement—rather than confound—each other.

Another Perspective on the Complementary Nature of Engineering and Design

Tom Chi, Experience Lead, Google Special Projects—www.tomchi.com

Doug Bowman's departure from Google sparked much heated discussion in the design world. While most of the follow-up conversation was strongly partisan—some defending Doug's position, others saying that Google had it right—my take is that both stories are incomplete.

The underlying problem is that design is a holistic discipline, while data-analysis, applied dogmatically, is a reductive discipline. When they're combined improperly, serious friction ensues. But far from vowing to never interact, these two disciplines need each other tremendously. The designer brings perspective that helps to organize experiential systems at all scales, while metrics are key to validating and optimizing those perspectives. The problems arise when analysis is treated as the primary driver for invention—that's like setting a measuring tape on a drafting table and expecting it to design spectacular architecture—rest assured, the genius is not in the tape. To best illustrate this point, I'll put on two hats.

FELLOW ENGINEERS

From the engineer's standpoint, quantitative metrics are an obvious must-have. Used well, they offer an impartial mechanism for tracking how code/design changes affect performance. Against that backdrop, design is really best understood as a kind of multivariate optimization of extreme complexity. Even a simple two-column layout with borders and background colors, the possible mix of colors, borders, column widths, layouts, and so on is exponential. Engineers familiar with large-scale optimization, even with approaches like max-descent, simulated annealing, and random restart, find that it's difficult to ensure that their customers are not trapped in local optima.

Think of your designer as a guide in this multivariate optimization process. A good designer has been all over parts of the territory a dozen times on various projects and has studied the design patterns and techniques that help in different problems/situations. Because of this, he intuitively knows how to approach a problem, just as an experienced software architect intuitively knows what software design approaches will provide various benefits/drawbacks. Don't think of this as some sort of "design mystique" with the designer projecting his "artist soul" or anything like that. A talented designer is similar to a senior technical architect because both can help you avoid configurations/combinations that are just not viable. Both the designer's and architect's designs are holistic, just as many good software architectures and system designs are holistic.

DEAR DESIGNERS

Okay, first off—design is not the same as art. In teaching seminars, I've often shared that "Art is about freedom; design is about constraints." Among the key constraints is the performance of your design, especially with respect to how it impacts your product and your business. While metrics may be scary to some, becoming familiar with different evaluation techniques and knowing which to employ are the hallmark of an experienced designer. The key is to extend your design process beyond the drawing of pixels, vectors, and boxes-and-arrows, to the design of the system within which your work is produced and evaluated. Once you are comfortable with a wide variety of evaluation techniques, you'll know which one will help clarify your key design decisions, and which will just waste your time only to produce noise. Instead of resisting or fearing evaluation of your design, you'll appropriately lift the conversation up to the level where you are discussing and proposing the right methods of evaluation.

This attitude won't turn a company's culture around overnight, but being the type of designer who knows how to validate and defend his designs will raise the value and respect of the discipline within your organization.

CONCLUSION

The interplay of all disciplines (engineering, design, research, marketing, sales, QA, product, legal, customer care, and so on) is where the magic happens. Metrics are an absolutely critical interface between disciplines, but when controlled and wielded by only one discipline, they can greatly limit the potential of the others. An organization that empowers only engineers will primarily produce engineering innovation, while an organization whose designers fear metrics will never reach the full potential of design. It is the organizations where all disciplines are represented and where metrics build common understanding that are able to innovate in several spheres at once, and those places will be vastly strengthened by this diversity.

Example 1: A Field Study Demystifies Site Search Analytics Data

We love this example; it's based on the experience of User Interface Engineering's Jared Spool. Imagine you're a WA person for a retailer, and while perusing your site's query data, you've discovered something strange: customers are searching SKU numbers—each product's unique identification number. This wouldn't seem so bizarre except for the fact that there are no SKUs featured in the site's catalog. So where are customers finding the SKUs? And *why* on earth would they use them?

While you may have some hypotheses, there's simply no way to find definitive answers from the analytics data. Fortunately, you have some UX colleagues to turn to. Their suggestion is to do a field study, where those customers can be observed interacting with the Web site in their natural habitat.

They return from the field with some interesting observations: customers don't only use the Web site; they also rely upon something else your company provides: a good old-fashioned printed catalog. In fact, they prefer this handy, familiar, and extremely high resolution catalog to the Web site when it comes to browsing for products. But ordering is so much easier on the Web site, and it avoids the messy business of interacting with other humans. So customers go online and search for the SKUs to fill their shopping cart as quickly and painlessly as possible.

Of course, if the site's product pages don't include SKUs, that experience won't be so quick and painless. But at least the SKU phenomenon identified by the WA folks is now understood—and, thanks to the field study, a traditional UX method, it can be easily addressed.

Example 2: Segmentation Leads to Better Personas

Now imagine that you're a UX person who is trying to get personas developed, accepted, and used by your Web team. But, not surprisingly, you're finding some resistance; after all, aren't these personas all just fiction? The developers shake their heads when you describe such a touchy-feely way of driving the design process!

Well, personas have a basis in truth—it's just that this "truth" is grounded in a qualitative (and often anecdotal) understanding of your site's audiences. In effect, personas are interpretations of interpretations. But if you could introduce "hard" data into persona development, you might reduce concerns with the "fictional" nature of personas.

Do that by asking your WA counterparts to show you their audience segmentation reports. These reports describe actual user behavior—the "what" of each segment. If you're fortunate, the segments will match up well with your personas; if not, you'll have to do some extrapolation.

After you've identified relevant segments, integrate their data as best you can into your personas to make them more concrete (see Figure 11.3). For example, that segment's common search queries can be used to illustrate a particular persona's common information needs and interests. Does funnel analysis show where a segment is failing? Incorporate this data as an example of what frustrates that persona when it uses your site.

Persona Chart:
Steven (Contractor)

Basic Information	
Age	36
Occupation	Design/Build Remodeler, CGR. He's been working in residential construction for nine years.
Net usage	30 mins to an hour a day, mostly for email, as well as some research for work.
Gear	Desktop Wintel PC, standard issue. Palm Vx for addresses, notes, calendaring, and time tracking.
Familiarity/Anxiety	Steven is comfortable using the computer and the Web for job-related needs. He's familiar with 3D House Designer, and a regular visitor at HousingZone.com.

Project Specific	
Trigger for action	Responding to client call... Not so much "triggered" as it is Steven's job.
Ultimate Goal	To make the client very happy with a kitchen remodel while pocketing a sizable profit.
Factors impacting availability	Also working on remodeling a condominium to ease an elderly person's living situation Taking a 2-week vacation 5 weeks into the project.
Estimated time for project	10 weeks
People needed to interact with	Clients, interior decorator, workmen, colleagues

How Steven Works	
Business situation	Is wholly independent—builds teams as needed
Working environment	Rents a small office, which he shares with 3 other people in the design/build industry.
Preferences for interacting with Others	Face-to-face is the best, followed by phone. Steven is a good, attentive talker. He dislikes email—a learning disability makes it quite time-consuming, and he's not confident about his writing skills.
What Steven Searches	award-winning remodelers top remodelers remodeling trends managing subcontractors site safety requirements

FIGURE 11.3
A data-infused persona, with associated queries ("What Steven Searches") added at the bottom. (Based on a persona from Adaptive Path.)

And there you have it: a traditional UX design tool (personas) was improved by a traditional WA tool (segmentation).

Example 3: Analytics as a Low-Cost Form of User Research

So what happens when you don't have the time or money for traditional user research? Analytics can help you diagnose the problem quickly. This example is based on some excellent work by Fred Beecher from Evantage Consulting. In this example, you're a UX consultant whose client's Web site appears to be failing. Your client knows this because it keeps hearing complaints from both customers and business partners. The client's industry is highly competitive, and product orders are often won or lost on customer service alone. But the client doesn't have the time or money for you to do the usability testing you know you need to do to identify the problems to focus on during user research. What do you do?

Look to your counterparts in web analytics. They may already have some data you can use to diagnose the problem. Collaboration with an analyst is key here. Analysts can help UX designers understand site traffic and query data. In this situation, Fred found very quickly that users were suffering from two big problems. Site traffic analysis revealed that users were looking for information all over the site. Search log analysis revealed that users were looking for very specific pieces of information. However, the search log also revealed that the terms users were searching on were close to, but did not exactly match, the syntax for those terms on the site. This led to many queries with no results, even though the information users were seeking was actually on the site.

Obtaining these insights required a little over three days. During that time, Fred and the rest of the team also conducted a series of extremely short guerilla interviews with friends in a related industry. Combining the insights gained from site traffic and search log analysis with those gained from the short interviews, the team was able to craft a streamlined user research plan. This plan allowed the team to focus on the problem areas during interviews and contextual inquiries, just like diagnostic usability testing would have. However, even a quick usability test takes at least two weeks to craft, schedule, and execute. The approach of combining analytics with guerrilla interviews yielded the same results in under a week.

Example 4: When Your Funnel's Broken, Task Analysis Can Explain Why

Now you're a WA person who works for a professional association, which is trying hard to expand its membership (traditionally based in the U.S.) into other countries. The association has made a big marketing push, which has resulted in more overall traffic, but hasn't led to the hoped-for bump up in registrations. When you perform funnel analysis on the registration process, you can see that visitors from non-U.S. IP addresses are getting tripped up on the page where they're supposed to enter their address information.

Now, many WA folks would say that their work is complete at this point— they've identified that there is, indeed, a problem and can point to *where* it's happening.

But the problem hasn't been solved because no one has determined *why* those users are failing. Does the problem have to do with translation? U.S.-address biased text entry boxes? A text entry sequence that assumes top-to-bottom and left-to-right? A page flow that makes sense for North Americans but not for East Asians? Or something else?

The answer won't come out of analytics data. However, there are a variety of methods—such as task analysis and field testing—that a UX person could apply to determine why the process is failing and how it might be fixed. For example, while subjects "think out loud" during a task analysis session, they may indicate that they're getting foiled by something as easy to fix as an insufficient number of address entry boxes to accommodate most non-North American street addresses (which can be quite long).

With help from your UX colleagues, you've closed the loop to make your analysis truly actionable, and together you've determined *what* is going on and *why*. And once the problem is diagnosed, the fix is cheap and easy to make.

To summarize: funnel analysis, a fixture of WA, was used to identify a major problem; a traditional UX method, task analysis, was then used to diagnose and address that problem.

Example 5: Finding Data to Back Up and De-Politicize Your Design

You're a UX person who is trying to figure out how wide your search box should be. It needs to squeeze into the header you'll be including in new templates used to generate every page in the site. Naturally, the owners of other features are clamoring for their own favorites to fit into that limited space, and the senior vice presidents among them are wielding their political power to get their way.

Rather than letting politics drive the design process (and, in the process, ending up with a tiny search box or, worse, a link to a separate search page), you enlist your WA counterpart to help. She has the data, and she can do the math. Together, you decide to actually measure the ideal length of your site's queries, using the method described in Chapter 8, "Practical Tips for Improving Search."

And—voilà!—now you have some real data to refer to when making your case. And you can even be a little Machiavellian in how you proceed. Perhaps you ask for a 12-character-wide query entry box, knowing that if you ended up with, say, 10, you'd still accommodate 60% of all your queries. (I'd actually suggest requesting a few more characters, given that these numbers are based on averages.) Either way, you've managed to work together with a web analytics person to come up with real behavioral data to justify an important design decision.

Each of these examples combines the *what* and *why* to form a sum that is greater than its parts. Sounds like a great idea, but doing so has typically been difficult: most of today's WA and UX people work in separate silos, using different tools to generate different types of research. Fortunately, the walls are starting to come down, as more and more intelligent organizations are enjoying the benefits of synthesizing their research—not just WA and UX, but from CRM, tech support, customer support, and other areas as well.

Creating a Single User Research Brain Within Your Organization

There are many more potential ways to integrate different research practices and, ultimately, make decisions with a whole brain. How can you get your own organization to start making its decisions with a full brain? The answer depends upon whom you are within your organization—a rank-and-file practitioner or a senior decision maker. So naturally, we'll explore the issue from both the bottom up and the top down.

From the Bottom Up: Grass Roots Organizing

If you're down in the trenches, your options are limited, but don't underestimate the gains that can be made from small, simple steps. Here are a few things you can do today.

Who's Out There?

You're looking to combine your data, analysis, and insights with those of the rest of your organization. So start by taking an inventory: who knows what within your organization's user research silos? You want to learn the following information:

- **What types of data they own?** Is it statistical or semantic? Logs or lab-generated? Behavioral or attitudinal? Aualitative or quantitative?

- **What sorts of tools and approaches do they use to learn from their data?** Do they rely upon Omniture to capture and analyze their data? Do they have a team of ethnographers analyzing transcripts from field studies? Do they have access to a statistician?

- **What types of insights do they use these data for?** Are they generating new product features or monitoring existing products' performance?

- **Which decision makers use these data?** Senior managers? Product managers? Advertising staff?

- **Who's doing the actual work?** What kinds of practitioners actually do the heavy lifting? What sorts of academic backgrounds do they come from? Do they have incentives to collaborate with you?

You won't likely be able to capture a complete picture of all the user- or customer-facing research activities in your organization—you wouldn't likely have time for that anyway. But if you can get a start, you—and whomever you enlist to join you—can fill in the blanks over time.

To get you started, you might begin with these potential sources within your organization:

- User research groups

- Web analytics groups

- Market research groups

- Product groups that maintain their own research teams

- Customer support/call center groups and switchboard operators

- Customer relationship management (CRM) groups

- Corporate library/research centers

You should also inventory the consultants and agencies that are involved in one type of user research or another; often, they know more about your users' behaviors than your own organization does.

Once you have a sense of who is out there, you're ready for the next step: lunch.

Let's Do Lunch

Invite a colleague to lunch to discuss her user research and to share your own. Go into your meeting having at least taken an initial pass at trying to fit your work with hers, as you've seen in the examples in the last section.

When you meet, try to get a little brainstorming going on how your insights might support each other's. For example, if you're a UX person, take the opportunity to learn from your WA counterpart more about your organization's KPI and then brainstorm together what sorts of qualitative data might strengthen those KPIs. If you're a WA person, learn about the design challenges that your UX colleagues face. Are there places where quantitative data could strengthen their decision-making process (for example, the personas example earlier) or the cases they need to make (as in the query entry box example)?

At the end of your lunch, offer to pick up the tab, ask to add your colleague to your LinkedIn network, and don't expect much to happen, at least right away. One-on-one connections are often the start of great movements, and small steps can be meaningful. You're just planting seeds right now.

Brown Bagging It

After you've had say, five lunches with new colleagues, you may be ready to start a brown bag series on the organization's user research. Be sure to invite others involved in any flavor of user research. Initially, your topics can center on simple reviews by representatives of your organization's different user research silos, covering the methodologies used and the kinds of insights gathered. As things pick up steam, invite outside experts to speak at your brown bags; not only will your organization's researchers benefit, but your brown bag will also gain a much higher profile.

If your brown bags gain some traction—with enough momentum that they can operate without your personal involvement—congratulations. You've succeeded in creating a community of interest around user research. This alone would be quite an achievement—it's a great step toward your organization's forming a complete user research brain.

But to make a real difference, grass roots movements can only go so far. There are typically few or no incentives to share information or collaborate with people in different silos within an organization. They can have lunch or go to a brown bag, but they won't be given the green light to spend the kind of time that's required to truly integrate and derive value from the various centers of user research. If you want to go further, senior leadership must buy into the plan.

From the Top Down: Involving Senior Leadership

Senior leaders are decision makers. If that's you, what kinds of data do you need to help you make the decisions that determine your organization's strategy? Play along for a moment: forget the acronyms, products, platforms, and practices that are floating around out there to describe user research. In fact, consider banning such words from your discussion altogether; terms like "CRM," "user research," and "Omniture" are so laden with baggage that they can obscure the critical goal: making well-informed decisions.

Okay, now ask yourself: what do *you* need to make good decisions?

Blue Skying the Organizational Brain

There won't likely be a single answer. Rather, you'll probably want a balanced diet of data, starting with a mix of quantitative and qualitative. You'll want data that describe users' actual behaviors, as well as their expressed attitudes. You'll want data that help you monitor performance so you stay true to your organization's goals, but you'll also want data that help suss out new trends and surprises—the stuff that changes your understanding of how your organization interacts with its audiences. Of course, you'll want to know *what* and you'll want to know *why*. And you'll want to synthesize all this good stuff so that the *sum is greater than the parts*.

In effect, you're developing an *organizational research agenda* to support your decision making. Your research agenda is made up of these components:

- The critical questions that you need answers for in order to make decisions.

- A broad and balanced set of data inputs to synthesize in order to answer those questions.

- A collection of tools and methods to help you obtain the data you need.

Figure 11.4 presents a variety of user research inputs as a landscape of inputs.[6] This isn't the only way to see the big picture—other axes could have been used, other research methods could and should have been included—but it's a great start.

---

6 This diagram is from Christian Rohrer's guest article in Useit.com, "When to Use Which User Experience Method" (October 6, 2008). It's also been attributed to Mulder and Yaar in *The User Is Always Right: A Practical Guide to Creating and Using Personas for the Web* (New Riders, 2006).

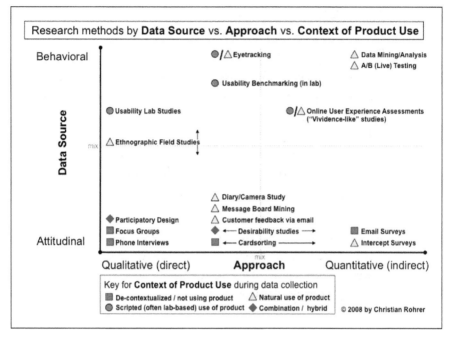

FIGURE 11.4

The Landscape of User Research Methods demonstrates both the diversity and complementary nature of the methods used by many different research fields.

As this research diagram comes from UX people, it's skewed toward the methods they tend to use. If a business analyst were to draw his research methods landscape, it would certainly look different. But I'm showing it because I want those responsible for an organization's decisions to consider: how would they draw this diagram for their whole organization?

The Decision-Making Dashboard

Developing a holistic view of your organization's research needs will help you in many ways: you'll find opportunities to eliminate redundancies, but you'll also identify gaps and correct imbalances in the tools, methods, and data that are currently driving your decision-making process. You'll also come up with ways to better sequence your user research. So imagine, if you will, a research "dashboard" that would include inputs from all of your research sources—in effect, an inventory of all of your organization's user research sources.

Consider taking things one step further and showing the relationships between those inputs. So, for example, draw a line between the "dial" for frequent search queries and the "dial" for your regular task analysis studies, as task analyses can be greatly informed by common queries. Not only does that mean both inputs are better, but as you draw lines showing the relationships between *all* of your data inputs, you'll also achieve true synthesis.

Finally, by starting with a unified research agenda, you'll find ways of better utilizing the smart, expensive people—in-house and consultants—who are already in your employ. If you can break down the silos that divide them, they'll be able to understand your organization's challenges *together* and execute on them *together*. Otherwise, all they're doing is understanding and executing incomplete solutions to incomplete problems.

Site Search Analytics: The Natural Boundary Object

So what does all our cheerleading for integrating different types of research have to do with site search analytics?

Well, SSA might be the best hope of bringing them together because it's a natural *boundary object*. According to Wikipedia, "Boundary objects are objects which are both plastic enough to adapt to local needs and constraints of the several parties employing them, yet robust enough to maintain a common identity across sites."[7] In our case, of course, the parties are web analytics and user experience.

I learned about boundary objects from visual thinker extraordinaire, Dave Gray, of XPLANE and author of *Gamestorming*. After mulling over the differences between "data people" and "design people," Dave naturally drew a picture (and shared some brilliant thoughts about how different disciplines

---

7   http://en.wikipedia.org/wiki/Boundary_object

can intersect).[8] Rather than portraying a simple boundary object, he took the concept further and drew a boundary matrix, as shown in Figure 11.5.

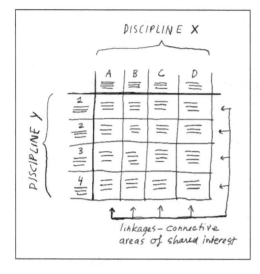

FIGURE 11.5

Dave Gray's boundary matrix shows how to link two disciplines (in our case, web analytics and user experience).

For example, data people might think in terms of segments; design people might think in terms of personas. Data people might think in terms of KPIs, while designers might think about goals. SSA has relevance to both: it can help augment both personas and traditional segments.

And its metrics can help connect goals and KPIs. Because of that mutual relevance, SSA itself is a boundary object that can offer a path that can connect data and design people. Consider this: almost all of the data that web analytics people work with is statistical. While clickstream data and site traffic data display users' behaviors, they're ultimately weak, as I've noted, at showing users' intentions and motives—at explaining "why" they do the things they do.

Site search query data is a very different kind of data: it's semantically rich in a way that no other analytic data comes close to. Queries are an almost pure expression of users' intentions and needs in their own words. The

---

8   Dave had some great observations on the topic; see www.gogamestorm.com/?p=58

closest competitor—analyzing navigation paths from clickstream data—helps you infer where users hope to go, but requires quite a lot of guessing. SSA requires little or no guessing at all about intent. So SSA plugs a huge attitudinal hole in web analytics' grasp of user intent.

Conversely, UX people have often been challenged to come up with the numbers to justify their design decisions. It's not enough to simply intuit that a "campus map" would be valuable to feature on a university's main page. It's not necessarily enough to have this intuition validated by test subjects in a laboratory environment. Thanks to SSA, you can now argue this point with much more certainty, and more importantly, with a much greater volume of data based upon actual usage to back you up. And you can justify how you label that information, as well as many other heretofore mushy design decisions that wilted under scrutiny from your organization's managers and other competing interests.

Really, SSA, with its connections to both user experience and web analytics, is the ideal *boundary object* for bringing them together. In other words, SSA should appeal to both WA and UX people. They may see its value differently, and use different terms to understand it, but nevertheless SSA offers value to both. So I'm hopeful that SSA can provide a beachhead for collaboration between smart analytics and UX people that might eventually enable organizations to make decisions with a full brain.

You may not use SSA for such ambitious goals as bridging entirely separate worlds of research and insight like web analytics and user experience. But I do hope you'll use it to improve your site's user experience in practical and meaningful ways, from making your search box wide enough to convincing your site's content owners to follow titling guidelines. SSA really does plug a gap in the conversations that organizations can have with their customers: where search queries express their information needs, analyzing query data makes sure you're answering those needs effectively. Good luck!

Index

SYMBOLS

80/20 Rule, 19

A

acronyms, 132, 136
Ad Service, income from, 114
ads, on search results pages, 66
Advanced Search, 130–132
AIGA, 100, 147
   search exit percentages, 72–74
airlines, searches, 133
Allen, Sarah, 104
Amazon, 113
AND Boolean operator, 125
Angel, Gary, 133–135
answer patterns, 50–52
anti-pattern analysis, 55
AOL researchers, and privacy, 93
Applications content type, 51
archive of search logs, 31
audience analysis, 23, 96–108.
   See also segmenting audience
audience segmentation reports, 173
auto-completion of queries, 127–128
average order, for segmenting
   audience, 100
awareness of SSA, lack of, 23
A–Z site indices, 148

B

base forms, converting words to, 45
BBC, 159
Beecher, Fred, 174
Belam, Martin, 139–141
best bets, 126–127
best match, location in search
   results, 70–71
bidding on keywords, 90
Big Book of Key Performance
   Indicators (Peterson), 115

Boolean operators, 124
boundary matrix to link
   disciplines, 183
boundary objects, 182
Bowman, Doug, 167, 168, 170
branding products, 161
broad terms, vs. metadata, 90
brown bag series on user research, 179

C

Card, Stuart, 130
case study on SSA, 2–12
Central Michigan University
   campus climate improvement as
      goal, 110
Chi, Tom, 170–171
cleaned-up queries for auto-complete,
   128
clickstream data, 71, 169
commerce sites, goals, 113
commercial databases, 124
Connors, Christine, 158
Contact info pages content types, 51
content
   available but not found, 67
   changing owners' actions, 162–163
   decision to remove, 156
   disconnect with site users, 67
   increasing relevance, 158–159
   plugging gaps, 156–158
   search results design around
      specialized types, 137–138
   search site analytics and, 22
   types for answers to queries, 51
   understanding user interests,
      159–161
content-rich sites, goals, 114
content strategy, 43
contextual navigation, 144–148

conversions, and audience
    segmentation, 100
converting words to base forms, 45
cookies, for user information, 17
costs of analytic tools, 24
Count, of query frequency, 40
Cumulative Percent, 40
Cutroni, Justin, 63

D

dashboard, decision making, 181–182
data, 183
    and design, 166–168
    legal hurdles to accessing, 24
    raw, for site search analytics, 16–18
databases, commercial, 124
dates, in searches, 136
date/time stamp for data, 17
Daylight Savings Time, 29
decision making dashboard, 181–182
design
    data and, 166–168
    engineering and, 170–171
    politics and, 176
desire paths, 145

E

empty queries, 57
engineering, design and, 168, 170–171
error messages, 129
ESPN, 114
Evantage Consulting, 174
Excel, 36
exit, queries resulting in
    immediate, 72–74, 116
Exploratory Data Analysis, 36
extended log entry, 28

F

failure analysis, 23, 62–78
    in audience analysis, 104
    caveats, 62–63
    meaningful failure, 74
    queries not retrieving useful results,
        68–72
    queries resulting in immediate exits,
        72–74
    queries with zero results, 63–67
failure, sessions ending in, 90
Ferrara, John, 68
field study, 169
funnel analysis, 175
fuzzy search, 45

G

garbage, in search log, 59
generic reports, for failure analysis, 62
geography, for segmenting
    audience, 100
GetSatisfaction.com, 114
GMT offset, 29
goal-based analysis, 110–120
goals
    determining, 113–118
    tracking, 110–113
Google, 124, 167, 170
Google AdWords, bid on
    keywords, 90
Google Analytics, 17, 24, 72, 125
    and audience segmentation, 99
    null results reports from, 63
    pivot feature, 101
Google Documents, spreadsheet, 36
Google Search Appliance, 16, 18
granularity of terms, session analysis
    and, 90–91
grass roots organizing, 177–179

Gray, Dave, 182, 183
guardian.co.uk Web site, 139–141

H

hacking of search engine, 58
Hewlett Packard, search engine, 137
hierarchy for site, 50
Hurst, Marko, 115
hyphenation, impact on searching, 45

I

identification numbers, 132
income, generating by content site, 114
indexes for sites, A to Z, 148
indexing by search engine, 67
  plugging gaps in, 122
information architect, 3
information need, change during
  session, 84
Instructions content type, 51
integrated problem solving, 168–176
intent of user, 62
Internal Revenue Service, Advanced
  Search interface, 131
internal testing queries, as log junk, 59
Irrelevant (i) rating, 69

J

jargon, 161
Jarrett, Caroline, 104
JavaScript code, for data capture, 17

K

Kaushik, Avinash, Web Analytics: An
  Hour a Day, 115
KPIs (Key Performance Indicators),
  22, 110–113
  determining, 113–118
  for searches, 112–113

L

language
  jargon, 161
  of users, vs. content, 41
  of users, vs. metadata, 150
  queries segmented by type, 101
  search vs. content, 67
lead generation sites, 114
legal hurdles for SSA, 24
LendingTree.com, 114
LEN function, 123
library catalogs, 124
logs. See search logs
long tail, 5, 19
  finding patterns in, 52–55
long tail analysis, 106
Loose relevance rating score, 69
loyalty, for segmenting audience, 100
lunch meetings with colleagues,
  178–179

M

marketing, 161–162
meaningful failure, 74
metadata, 22, 67, 158
  applying, 90
  and auto-complete list, 128
  creating set, 42
  eliminating terms, 153
  testing and tuning, 150–153
  tracking trends, 152–153
metrics
  based on query data, 115–118
  for common queries, 5
  for current search engine
    experience, 4
  for junk log entries, 59
  vs. KPIs, 110
  for precision, 9, 10, 11
  quantitative, 170

for relevancy, 9, 10, 11
for searches, 112–113
Michigan State University, 148, 157
PERL script from, 17
Microsoft.com, content, 156
Microsoft Excel, 36
Microsoft Support, 114
Misplaced (m) rating, 69
Morningstar.com, 64
Mortensen, Dennis, 110

N

National Cancer Institute, 126
natural boundary object, 182–184
navigation, 22
contextual, 144–148
Navigation pages content type, 51
NCSA extended Web server log
format, 27
Near (n) rating, 68
needs of searcher, 83
Netflix, 74–76
News and Announcements content
type, 51
New York Times, 114
Nielsen, Jakob, 21
"No Results Found" page,
improving, 129–130
Norton (WW), session analysis,
86–89
NOT Boolean operator, 125
noun phrases, 44
Nudelman, Greg, 64–66
null results reports, 63.
See also zero results queries

O

Omniture, 17
OpenOffice, spreadsheet, 36
Open University, 104–106

OR Boolean operator, 125
organization
research agenda, 180
unique audience segments, 103
organizational brain, 180–184
organizational sites, types, 113
organization names, 136
outliers, 6, 56, 147

P

page design, and thrashing, 64
page views, 116
Pareto Principle, 19
parsing queries, PERL script for, 36
patent information, zero results query
and, 62
pattern analysis, 23, 34–60
answer patterns, 50–52
anti-pattern analysis, 55
as form of play, 34–36
in audience analysis, 104
considerations, 40–52
finding patterns in long tail, 52–55
getting started, 36–40
question patterns, 48–50
synonym patterns, 41–43
tonal patterns, 41
percentage of overall search activity,
for each query, 37
PERL script
for parsing data, 17
for parsing queries, 36
Permissive relevance rating score, 69
personal names, 135
personas, 97, 172–174
Peterson, Eric T., The Big Book of Key
Performance Indicators, 115
phrase queries, 44–45
Pirolli, Peter, 130
place names, 136

policies and procedures, 162–163
politics
  and design, 176
  hurdles for SSA, 24
  in recommended links selection, 127
Power Laws, 19
precision, 5, 7–9
  metrics, 9, 10, 11
preferred term, analysis to
  determine, 43
privacy protection, 81
problem solving, integrated, 168–176
proper noun phrase, 44
proper nouns, 132

Q

quantitative metrics, 170
queries, 183
  alphabetical index built around, 148
  analysis, 5–9
  classification by users, 88
  customization, 133–135
  empty, 57
  motivations for revising, 131
  rank by frequency, 37
  repeat, 57
  search metrics based on, 115–118
  on SKU numbers, 172
  starting point for, 144, 146
  text-entry box for, 122–124
  user differences, 98
  zero results, 22, 63–67.
    See also zero results queries
query test, for metadata, 150–151
Quesenbery, Whitney, 104
question patterns, 48–50

R

random sample, for long tail pattern
  analysis, 53

Rappoport, Avi, 27, 57–59
rating results, scale for precision
  testing, 7–8
raw data, for site search analytics,
  16–18
real estate sites, searches, 133, 134
recommended links, 126–127
Reference pages content type, 51
"referer" field, 28
registration process, 175
regular expressions, 58
relevance, 5–7
  to business, 67
  limitations of testing, 7
  metrics, 9, 10, 11
  of content, increasing, 158–159
  of query results, 4, 68–70
  for phrase queries, 44
  ranking algorithm weighting
    configuration, 86
Relevant (r) rating, 68
repeat queries, 57
reports, 21
reverse lookup, 151–152
robot crawlers, 58
Rohrer, Christian, 180
ROT (Redundant, Outdated, and
  Trivial) content, 156

S

Sandia National Labs, 162
scent of information, 130
Search conversion rate, 117
search engine
  indexing by, 67
  metrics for current experience, 4
  performance comparison, 9
  planned launch, 2
  plugging gaps in index, 122
  transaction logs for, 27
  troubleshooting, 3

searchers. *See* users
searches
  data availability vs. privacy, 93
  goal setting and, 110
  metrics and KPI, 112–113
  page originating, 144
  parameters in log entry, 30
search field spam, 58
search improvement, 122–142
  accommodating strange
      syntax, 124–125
  auto-completion, 127–128
  best bets, 126–127
  "No Results Found" page
      improvement, 129–130
  plugging gaps in search engine's
      index, 122
  results design around specialized
      content types, 137–138
  results design around specialized
      query types, 132–137
  revisions for better results, 130–132
  text-entry box, 122–124
search log analysis, 174
search log entry
  anatomy, 27–31
  basic fields, 27
  extended, 28
search logs, 17
  removing junk, 59
  taxonomy of junk, 57–59
  URLs in, 137
search queries. *See* queries
Search refinement rate, 117
search results, best match
    location, 70–71
search scoping, site search analytics
    and, 139–141
seasonality, of information usage, 46
segmentation, 172–174

segmenting audience, 96–99
  benefits, 97
  comparing and contrasting, 104
  process, 99–104
selection rate metric, 71
SelectQuote.com, 114
self-service/support sites, 114
SEM (Search Engine Marketing), 32
senior leadership, in user research
    integration, 179–184
SEO (Search Engine
    Optimization), 32, 90
server hacks, 58
session analysis, 23, 80–94
  in audience analysis, 104
  for failed sessions, 90
  granularity of terms, 90–91
  reasons, 83
  selecting sessions for, 89–90
  TFANet example, 84–86
  who, what, and when, 80–82
  WW Norton long session, 86–89
sessions
  average # queries, 116
  defining, 83–84
short head, 19
  focus on, 96
site indices, improving, 148–154
site search analytics, 184
  basics, 14–16
  case study, 2–12
  importance of, 10
  natural boundary object, 182–184
  obstacles, 23–24
  raw data for, 16–18
  reasons to use, 16
  responsibility for, 25–26
  and search scoping, 139–141
  use options, 22–23
site search query data, 183

site traffic analysis, 174
SKU numbers, customer search of, 172
spam, search field, 58
spider, 58
Spool, Jared, 172
spreadsheet
  for data analysis, 17
  for pattern analysis, 36
  template use, 40
stemmer, 45
Stirling, Viki, 104
Strict relevance rating score, 69
style conventions, 162
subscription, income generation, 114
surveys, vs. query analysis, 113
synonym patterns, 41–43
synonyms, 153

T

tag cloud, 92
task analysis, 175
Teach For America, 80–82
technical hurdles for SSA, 24
template for spreadsheet, 37
  using, 40
terms. *See* vocabulary
testing metadata, 150–153
text-entry box, for query, 122–124
TFANet, 80–82
  session analysis example, 84–86
third-party resources, on search results
  pages, 66
thrashing, 64–66
time constraints of session, 84
time of day, and retail customer
  searches, 48
time zones, 29
timing, for segmenting audience, 100
titling documents, 158
tolerances, range for precision levels, 8

tonal patterns, 41
top-down analysis, 118
tracking goals, 110–113
traffic sources, for segmenting
  audience, 100
transaction logs, for search engine, 27
trends in metadata, tracking, 152
troubleshooting search engine, 3
type-ahead for queries, 127–128

U

Underwood, Walter, 44–45
Unica, 17
University of Alaska Fairbanks,
  Advanced Search interface, 131
URLs
  in query logs, 137
  search for, 55
usability test, 174
user-centered thinking, 4
user data. *See* data
user experience, 166, 184
  of search, 3
  web analytics vs., 168
user experience people, analysis by, 25
user information, cookies for, 17
User Interface Engineering, 144
user research
  brown bag series on, 179
  discussion over lunch, 178–179
  inputs, 180
  integrating, 177–182
  methods, 181
  web analytics as, 174–175
users
  analysis of sessions, 92–93
  characteristics, 68
  content disconnect with, 67
  intent of, 26, 62
  needs of, 83

query classification by, 88
query differences, 98
understanding content interest
of, 159–161

V

Vanguard Group, 68–70
vocabulary
adding new term to, 153
analysis to determine preferred
term, 43
converting words to base forms, 45
jargon, 161
session analysis and granularity of,
90–91
users vs. site, 174

W

Washtenaw Community College, 161
web analytics, 166, 184
as user research, 174–175
vs. user experience, 168

Web Analytics: An Hour a Day
(Kaushik), 115
Web Analytics Forum Yahoo Group, 25
width of search box, 123, 176
Wiggins, Rich, 15, 46
Wikipedia, 182
words. *See* vocabulary
writing quality, 158

Y

YouTube, 114

Z

zero results queries, 22, 63–67, 115
and indexing gaps, 122
patent information and, 62
reducing thrashing, 64–66
reviewing, 156
Zipf distribution, 19–21
Zipf, George Kingsley, 19–21

ACKNOWLEDGMENTS

I've heard it's lonely at the top. It also must be lonely at the (fore)front. I say that because the smartest people I know—the ones five or ten years ahead of the rest of us—are invariably the ones who are most willing to share what they know. Perhaps they're just dying for *someone* to see that they've stumbled upon a fantastic new way to solve a problem. Or maybe being brilliant and generous just go hand in hand.

Whatever it is, a few of those really smart people shared what they knew with me, and without them, this book wouldn't have happened. One was my old friend from Michigan, **Rich Wiggins**. He introduced me to site search analytics about 10 years ago. Rich knew that SSA could close a critical feedback loop in the user experience of search, and somehow managed to convince his bosses at Michigan State University to let him institute an SSA program. Today, MSU is one of the most successful institutional users of SSA, and many of this book's examples are a product of its—and Rich's—excellent work.

Rich's and my shared interest in SSA connected us with two other smart people, **Avi Rappoport** and **Walter Underwood**, who have both made short contributions to this book. If you're looking for people to analyze your query data, you won't find any better than Avi and Walter.

Like a lot of people in user experience, I'm very much a right-brain person, and I'm not entirely comfortable with data. **Marko Hurst** is one of those few people fortunate to function with a full brain. Marko can combine qualitative and quantitative analyses like no one I've met in the field, and he made sure this book took a far more balanced perspective on how to derive value from query data.

I was fortunate to have five tough technical reviewers who reflected a healthy variety of perspectives. **Steve Krug, Avi Rappoport, Vivian Bliss, John Godinez**, and **Anil Batra** were truly a dream team of practical advisors and healthy challengers; the book is much improved thanks to their efforts. And it benefited further from great contributions by these experts: **Gary Angel**, **Martin Belam**, **Tom Chi**, and **Greg Nudelman**.

A huge cadre contributed stories (and sometimes data) about their work for me to use in this book (most of which I used). They were often the same people who kept at me over too many years to get the book written, and I'm grateful to them: **Mary Ambrosio**, **Meredith Anderson**, **Ricardo Baeza-Yates**, **Jeannine Bartlett**, **Fred Beecher**, **Christopher Billick**, **Mandy Brown**, **Lorelei Brown**, **Christine Connors**, **Justin Cutroni**, **Richard Dalton**, **Liz Danzico**, **John Ferrara**, **Alexandra Fox**, **Manya Kapikian**, **Nick Finck**, **Zach Gemignani**, **Dave Gray**, **Steve Hatch**, **Jason Hibbets**, **Caroline Jarrett**, **Avinash Kaushik**, **Phil Kemelor**, **Neil Kohl**, **Chris Kutler**, **Jeff Lash**, **Fred Leise**, **Helen Lippell**, **Karen Loasby**, **Lydia Mann**, **Matthew Marco**, **Ravi Mynampaty**, **Cynthia Osiecki**, **Robert Piddocke**, **Whitney Quesenbery**, **Brendan Quinn**, **Susan Rogers**, **Shaun Ryan**, **Denise Shanks**, **Tito Sierra**, **Johnny Snellgrove**, **Jared Spool**, **Mike Steckel**, **R. Todd Stephens**, **Walter Underwood**, **Guy Valerio**, **Javier Velasco**, **Abbie Walsh**, **Jennifer Whalen**, **Denise Wood**, and **Jeffrey Zeldman**.

It's strange when the author is also the publisher. Yet everyone involved in the book's development and production made life easier for me, regardless of which hat I wore. It was an absolute joy to work with **Stephanie Zhong**, the book's developmental editor. Given that she is using SSA at her day job at Teach for America, she was the ideal editor to work with. (It also helps that she's very patient.) **Karen Corbett**, Rosenfeld Media's Director of Operations, helped me in more ways on a daily basis than I can recount. (She's also very patient.) And Rosenfeld Media's crack production team maintained its high standards in creating and assembling the final product; many, many thanks to **Marta Justak** (our managing editor), **Danielle Foster** (our interior designer), **The Heads of State** (who create our covers), **Chuck Hutchinson** (proofreader), and **Nancy Guenther** (indexer).

Finally, my wife, **Mary Jean Babic**, always looks at my new books' acknowledgments pages first—as well she should. She knows when she's owed big time, and this book—which took me forever to write—is such a case. Hopefully, **Iris** and **Nate** will inherit her genes for supportiveness and good counsel, rather than mine for procrastination and metaphor mixology.

I'm very glad that brilliant and generous often do go hand in hand.

Thanks all.

—Louis Rosenfeld
    Brooklyn, NY
    March, 2011

ABOUT THE AUTHOR

PHOTO BY MYRA KLARMAN
(HTTP://MYRAKLARMAN.COM/)

Lou Rosenfeld wears two hats.

As an information architecture consultant, he helps Fortune 500s and other large, highly political organizations make their messy information easier to find. His past clients include PayPal, Caterpillar, Ford, The Centers for Disease Control, SIGGRAPH, AT&T, and Borders. With Peter Morville, Lou co-authored *Information Architecture for the World Wide Web* (O'Reilly & Associates; 3rd edition, 2006), regarded as the bible of information architecture, and has been a regular contributor to *Web Review, Internet World*, and *CIO* magazines. Lou co-founded the Information Architecture Institute. He still blogs occasionally at www.louisrosenfeld.com.

As a publisher, Lou founded Rosenfeld Media, so that there would be at least one publishing house dedicated to serving the needs of the growing community of user experience practitioners. In its short life, the company has published such seminal titles as Luke Wroblewski's *Web Form Design* and *Storytelling for User Experience* by Whitney Quesenbery and Kevin Brooks. Lou's book is the eighth title that Rosenfeld Media has published, and about a dozen more should be available by 2013.

Lou holds a Masters in Information and Library Studies and a B.A. in History, both from the University of Michigan. He lives in Brooklyn, New York with his wife, Mary Jean Babic, their children, Iris and Nate, and two cats that don't seem to be even remotely interested in user experience.

TESTIMONIALS

"Search is one of those mission-critical aspects of every Web site that is sadly all too often forgotten until the damage has already been done. Lou, on the other hand, is one of those guys who understands search analytics and the opportunity associated with digging into the nuances of customer and search behaviors to mine for organizational gold. In *Search Analytics for Your Site*, Lou lays out pretty much everything you need to know to mine for that gold and convert it into a positive customer experience on your site."

—Eric T. Peterson, Founder and Author, *Web Analytics Demystified*

"Clients have asked me countless times to pretty up their search results page design, as if this would distract users from realizing that they're getting lousy results. That's no longer necessary, thanks to Lou's book."

—Karen McGrane, Managing Partner, Bond Art + Science

"At last a book that explains exactly how to get the best from search analytics so that users can actually find what they are looking for."

—Martin White, Managing Director, Intranet Focus Ltd, and author of *Making Search Work*

"Analytics are the single most important tool you have to improve your search experience, and Lou Rosenfeld's world-class expertise in user-centered design is the place to start."

—Pete Bell, co-founder, Endeca

"Louis Rosenfeld's *Search Analytics for Your Site* is a superlative work from the initial story to the final chapter on bridging web analytics and UX practice. I'm somewhat experienced with event logging methods, but Lou's book opened my mind to new ways to use analytics. Each chapter is packed with useful information, clear examples, and refreshing caveats that could only come from a master of search analytics. The book is written in an engaging style that makes you feel like Louis is with you on every page. I plan to apply some of the knowledge and techniques immediately. Great book!"

—Chauncey Wilson, Senior Manager, User Research

TESTIMONIALS

"If we all agree that user feedback will improve any site's user experience, why aren't we spending more time with the actual words our audience uses when asking us for stuff? I can't imagine a more experienced guide than Lou Rosenfeld to help us put this amazing data to work."

—Jeffrey Veen, Founder & CEO, Typekit

"Lou is the perfect author to tackle what is essentially unexplored territory in the UX community. With *Search Analytics for Your Site*, he has uncovered a huge goldmine for UX professionals of all stripes: now we have the tools to finally, finally fix our Web site and intranet search experiences. This is one of those rare books that makes me pound the table with my fist and yell, 'Yes! Exactly! Awesome!' while I'm reading it."

—Kristina Halvorson, CEO, Brain Traffic, and author, *Content Strategy for the Web*

"Lou Rosenfeld provides remarkable clarity, insight, and humor on the complicated world of search site analytics. *Search Analytics for Your Site* will no doubt be an indispensable resource for anyone involved in user experience and web analytics."

—Bill Albert, Ph.D, Director, Design and Usability Center, Bentley University

"The potential value behind the queries issued by your customers is in practice unbounded. So do not waste this potential—use the knowledge behind these queries. For that, you have to understand search analytics, and hence you must read this book."

—Ricardo Baeza-Yates, VP of Yahoo! Research

OTHER BOOKS FROM
🐘 ROSENFELD MEDIA

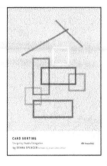

Card Sorting: Designing Usable Categories
by Donna Spencer
April 2009
1-933820-02-0

www.rosenfeldmedia.com/books/cardsorting

Card sorting is a user research technique that will help you design a usable information architecture for a Web site or intranet, and for any project that involves organizing content. Donna Spencer's book is short, practical, and accessible, and includes many case studies and real-life examples.

Web Form Design: Filling in the Blanks
by Luke Wroblewski
May 2008
1-933820-24-1

www.rosenfeldmedia.com/books/webforms

Web Form Design provides practical, research driven design recommendations for Web designers, developers, business managers, marketers, and more. The book covers Web form design for e-commerce, social software, intranets, Web applications, and Web sites.

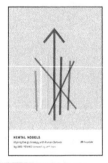

Mental Models: Aligning design strategy with human behavior
by Indi Young
February 2008
1-933820-06-3

www.rosenfeldmedia.com/books/mental-models

Mental models give you a deep understanding of people's motivations and thought processes, along with the emotional and philosophical landscape in which they are operating. You use mental models to align your design strategy with what people want.

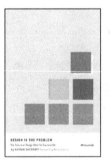

Design Is the Problem: The Future of Design Must be Sustainable
by Nathan Shedroff
March 2009
1-933820-00-4

www.rosenfeldmedia.com/books/sustainable-design

In *Design Is the Problem*, Nathan Shedroff examines how the endemic culture of design creates unsustainable solutions, and helps designers bake sustainability into their design processes.

OTHER BOOKS FROM  ROSENFELD MEDIA

Prototyping: A Practitioner's Guide
by Todd Zaki Warfel
November 2009
1-933820-21-7

www.rosenfeldmedia.com/books/prototyping

Prototypes help you to flesh out design ideas, test assumptions, and gather real-time feedback from users. Todd Zaki Warfel shows how prototypes are more than just a design tool by demonstrating how they can help you market a product, gain internal buy-in, and test feasibility with your development team.

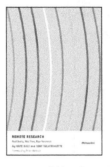

Remote Research: Real Users, Real Time, Real Research
by Nate Bolt &
Tony Tulathimutte
February 2010
1-933820-77-2

www.rosenfeldmedia.com/books/remote-research

Remote studies allow you to recruit subjects quickly, cheaply, and immediately, and give you the opportunity to observe users as they behave naturally in their own environment. In *Remote Research*, Nate Bolt and Tony Tulathimutte teach you how to design and conduct remote research studies, top to bottom, with little more than a phone and a laptop

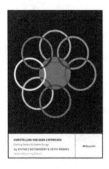

Storytelling for User Experience: Crafting Stories for Better Design
by Whitney Quesenbery and Kevin Brooks
April 2010
1-933820-47-0

www.rosenfeldmedia.com/books/storytelling/

We all use stories to communicate, explore, persuade, and inspire. In user experience, stories help us to understand our users, learn about their goals, explain our research, and demonstrate our design ideas. In this book, Quesenbery and Brooks teach you how to craft and tell your own unique stories to improve your designs.

UPCOMING BOOKS FROM
🐘 ROSENFELD MEDIA

Agile Experience Design
by Anders Ramsay, to be published 2011
🐘 www.rosenfeldmedia.com/books/agile-experience/

The Art and Craft of User Research Interviewing: Diving Deep for Insight
by Steve Portigal, to be published 2012
🐘 www.rosenfeldmedia.com/books/user-interviews/

Designing for Care: The Design Disciplines as Critical Healthcare Professions
by Peter Jones, to be published 2011
🐘 www.rosenfeldmedia.com/books/health-care/

Eye Tracking the User Experience: A Practical Guide
by Aga Bojko, to be published 2012
🐘 www.rosenfeldmedia.com/books/eye-tracking/

Make It So: Interaction Design Lessons from Science Fiction
by Nathan Shedroff & Chris Noessel, to be published 2012
🐘 www.rosenfeldmedia.com/books/science-fiction-interface/

The Mobile Frontier: A Guide for Designing Mobile Experiences
by Rachel Hinman, to be published 2011
🐘 www.rosenfeldmedia.com/books/mobile-design/

UPCOMING BOOKS FROM
🐘 ROSENFELD MEDIA

Playful Design: Creating Game
Experiences in Everyday Interfaces
by John Ferrara, to be published 2011
🐘 www.rosenfeldmedia.com/books/game-design/

See What I Mean: How to Use Comics
to Communicate Ideas
by Kevin Cheng, to be published 2011
🐘 www.rosenfeldmedia.com/books/comics/

Service Design: Designing Useful,
Usable, and Desirable Services
by Andy Polaine, Lavrans Løvlie, & Ben Reason, to be published 2012
🐘 www.rosenfeldmedia.com/books/service-design/

Surveys That Work
by Caroline Jarrett, to be published 2012
🐘 www.rosenfeldmedia.com/books/survey-design/

UX Team of One
by Leah Buley, to be published 2012
🐘 www.rosenfeldmedia.com/books/ux-team-of-one/

Universal Design for Web Accessibility:
Solutions for Barrier-Free User Experiences
by Sarah Horton & Whitney Quesenbery, to be published 2012
🐘 www.rosenfeldmedia.com/books/web-accessibility/

KEEP UP WITH
🐘 ROSENFELD MEDIA

We'd love to let you know of new book signings, discounts and promotions, author presentations, and other Rosenfeld Media news. There are plenty of ways to stay in touch:

- Subscribe to our free monthly newsletter, the Rosenfeld Review: is.gd/9viTRS

- Visit our site: 🐘 www.rosenfeldmedia.com

- Subscribe to our RSS feed: 🐘 feeds.rosenfeldmedia.com/rosenfeldmedia

- Follow us on Twitter: @rosenfeldmedia

- Email us: info@rosenfeldmedia.com

CPSIA information can be obtained
at www.ICGtesting.com
Printed in the USA
JSHW011523020723
43976JS00001B/2